The River Cafe Cookbook

Rose Gray and Ruth Rogers

EBURY PRESS • LONDON

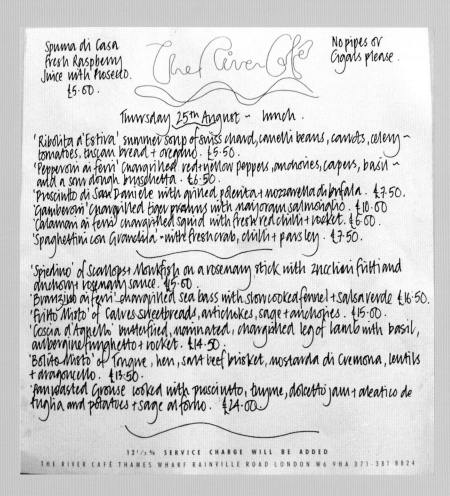

Photographs **Jean Pigozzi** with food photography by **Martyn Thompson**
designed by the **Senate**

Text copyright © Ruth Rogers and Rose Gray 1995. Photographs copyright © Jean Pigozzi and Martyn Thompson. Ruth Rogers and Rose Gray have asserted their right to be identified as the authors of this work. First published in 1995 by Ebury Press, Random House, 20 Vauxhall Bridge Road, London SW1V 2SA; Random House Australia (Pty) Limited, 20 Alfred Street, Milsons Point, Sydney, New South Wales 2061, Australia; Random House New Zealand Limited, 18 Poland Road, Glenfield, Auckland 10, New Zealand; Random House South Africa (Pty) Limited, PO Box 337, Bergvlei, South Africa. Random House UK Limited Reg. No. 954009. Printed and bound in Great Britain by Butler and Tanner Ltd, Frome and London. A CIP catalogue record for this book is available from the British Library. **ISBN 0-09-180731-X**

Contents

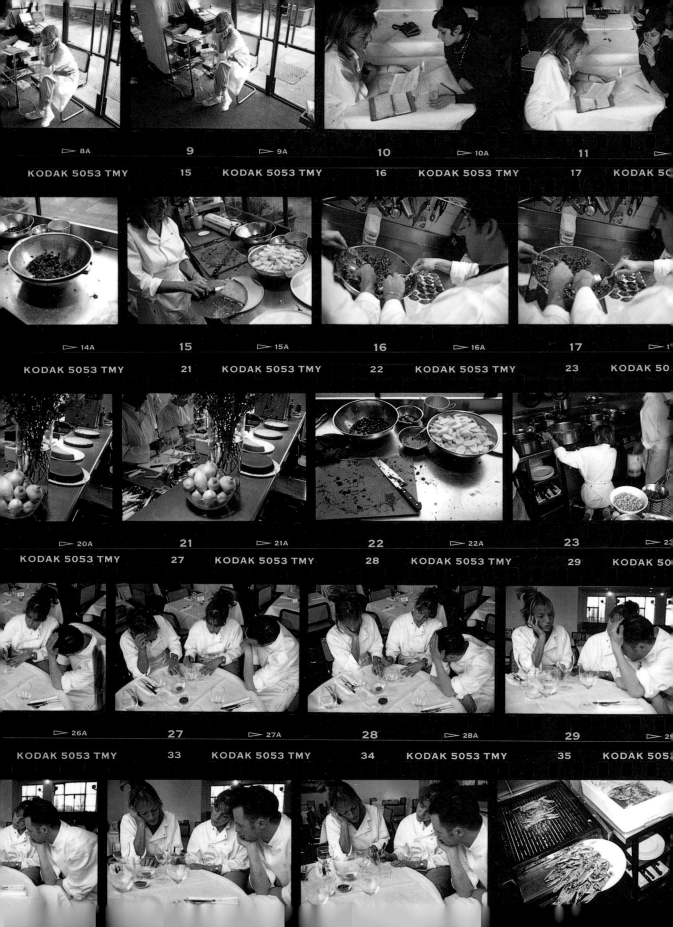

Introduction

The River Cafe opened in 1987. It was inspired and influenced by our experience of living and cooking in Italy. Both of us spent long periods in Tuscany, with family and friends, and learned an enormous amount by watching, tasting and experimenting as we went.

The ingredients themselves were a revelation. We were overwhelmed by the enormous variety of produce available in Italian food shops – the local pecorinos, the different types of prosciuttos and salamis, the smoked and salted pancettas, olive oils made by local farms, and olives preserved in brine. There were inviting sacks of dried beans – borlotti, fave, cannellini and ceci. In the vegetable markets we found tiny fennel bulbs which could be eaten raw, huge dense bunches of cicoria, stalls that sold only herbs, or garlic or wild leaves.

In Italy we learned about the importance of seasonality, robust flavours, the structure of a meal and the natural connection between a region's wine and its food. All this influenced the way we cooked and we transferred this knowledge and our enthusiasm directly to the restaurant.

Eight years ago obtaining the right ingredients was a challenge. We brought back seeds of cavolo nero from Italy and persuaded an organic gardener to grow them for us. In the garden on the riverbank outside the restaurant we experimented in planting Capri rocket, cultivating dandelion leaves, and growing a range of herbs which we could pick every day.

It is now much easier to obtain these ingredients – mozzarella is flown in from Naples once a week, one of our wine suppliers, Winecellars, imports olive oils, pasta and polenta flours as well as wine, and many of the vegetables are now available through specialist suppliers. We have provided a list of stockists, and we're sure that everyone using and reading this book should be able to obtain everything they need.

From the beginning we were confident that our ideals for a restaurant were the same. We shared a love for Italian food, we were both interested in the new restaurants opening then in California and New York, which looked towards rustic European cooking yet grafted onto this a certain American simplicity and directness. We were determined to have only Italian wines on our wine list. We were also convinced that we could extend the way we lived and cooked at home into the restaurant, and create a style that was natural and true to our own tastes. The River Cafe was conceived deliberately along domestic lines, with a small open kitchen, a menu that would change for every meal, and the unconventional idea that the waiters and kitchen porters would be involved in the preparation of the food.

We feel that our recipes are accessible to anyone cooking at home. We took our Italian knowledge and recipes from the domestic kitchen to the restaurant; our book now returns them there.

Rose Gray & **Ruth Rogers** London 1995

SoU

ups

1

What we love most about Italian soups is what we love most about Italian food. They are regional, seasonal and their ingredients are undisguised and definite.

You would be as unlikely to find a Pappa al Pomodoro served in a home or restaurant in Aosta as a Zuppa di Aosta in Tuscany. Both are soups of their region – Tuscans are proud of their bread, considering it more important than pasta and every garden has its row of tomatoes. In the high mountainous province of Aosta, the soups are filling and comforting – made with stock, salted anchovies, butter and Fontina cheese.

The seasonal quality of Italian soups is reflected in the method of cooking and the ingredients used. Dried cannelli are best in November and coincide with the arrival of the new oil, winter minestrones are dark green and cook for a long time. The soups of spring and summer are still strong and definite but lighter, fresher and more fragrant. Summer minestrone is a vivid green with an abundance of fresh herbs and hardly cooked young peas and asparagus.

Apart from the minestrones and fish stews, Italian soups have few ingredients. Our zucchini soup uses large quantities of zucchini and basil, whilst the cannellini bean soup is no more than parsley, garlic, cannellini beans and extra virgin olive oil.

Zuppa di Cozze in Bianco
White Mussel Soup

This mussel soup comes from the Ligurian coast. It is called bianco because, unusually for Italian fish soup, it contains wine and garlic, but no tomato.

Serves 6

2.5 kg (5.1/2 lb) mussels

75 ml (2.1/2 fl oz) olive oil

4 garlic cloves, peeled and chopped

1/2 bottle white wine

1 small dried chilli, crushed

1 bunch flat-leaf parsley, chopped

sea salt and freshly ground black pepper

Crostini

6 slices ciabatta bread, cut at an angle

1 garlic clove, peeled and halved

extra virgin olive oil

Clean the mussels very thoroughly under cold running water. Scrub well with a stiff brush, and scrape off any barnacles. Discard any that are open or have cracked or broken shells.

Heat 60 ml (2 fl oz) of the olive oil until very hot in the biggest pan you have, one with a tight-fitting lid. Add two-thirds of the chopped garlic; it will colour immediately. Throw in the mussels, put on the lid and shake the pan fiercely to coat the mussels with oil. Add the wine. Return to the heat, shake, cook and stir until all the mussels are open. This will only take a couple of minutes.

Put the opened mussels and their juices into a large bowl to cool, then remove half the mussels from their shells. Discard any that have not opened.

In the same pan heat the remaining olive oil and fry the rest of the garlic until light brown, then add the chilli, half the parsley and the liquid from the mussels. When hot, add all the mussels, shelled and unshelled, salt and pepper and most of the remaining parsley.

To make the crostini, toast the ciabatta slices on both sides, and rub with the garlic. Serve the soup in flat open dishes with the crostini and pour over a generous amount of extra virgin olive oil. Scatter with the remaining parsley.

Zuppa di Cozze Piccante
Spicy Mussel Soup

In its use of chillies, anchovies and tomatoes, this mussel soup from Puglia is typical of the southern Italian style of cooking.

Serves 6

2.5 kg (5.1/2 lb) mussels, cleaned as in the previous recipe

75 ml (2.1/2 fl oz) olive oil

150 ml (5 fl oz) white wine

4 garlic cloves, peeled and finely chopped

6 anchovy fillets

3 small dried chillies, crumbled

1 x 800 g (1.3/4 lb) tin peeled plum tomatoes, drained of most of their juices, chopped

sea salt and freshly ground black pepper

1 bunch flat-leaf parsley, chopped

Bruschetta

6 slices pugliese bread, cut at an angle

1 garlic clove, peeled and halved

extra virgin olive oil

Heat 60 ml (2 fl oz) of the olive oil in a large saucepan, then add the mussels, the white wine and 120 ml (4 fl oz) water. Cook over a high heat until all the mussels are open, discarding any that remain closed. You may need to cook the mussels in batches; divide the oil, wine and water accordingly.

Remove the mussels, and boil to reduce the liquid by half. Remove half the mussels from their shells.

Heat the remaining olive oil in a large pan and fry the garlic until lightly brown. Add the anchovies, and mash with the garlic into the hot oil until dissolved. Add the mussel liquid, the chilli and the tomatoes. Cook gently until the tomatoes have reduced to a medium-thick consistency. This should take about 30 minutes. Season with salt and pepper and more chilli if necessary. Finally, put in the mussels, shelled and unshelled, and half the parsley.

To make the bruschetta, toast the bread on both sides and rub with the garlic. Serve the soup in flat open dishes with the bruschetta, the remaining parsley and a generous amount of the very best extra virgin olive oil.

Zuppa Estiva di Cozze
Summer Mussel Soup

Serves 6

2.5 kg (5.1/2 lb) mussels, cleaned (see page 15)

120 ml (4 fl oz) olive oil

3 garlic cloves, peeled (2 in slivers, 1 chopped)

1 large bunch basil, stalks removed

1.25 kg (2.3/4 lb) ripe plum tomatoes, skinned, seeded and chopped, juices retained

sea salt and freshly ground black pepper

Bruschetta

6 slices ciabatta bread, cut at an angle

2 garlic cloves, peeled

extra virgin olive oil

Heat 4 tablespoons of the olive oil in a large, heavy saucepan, add the garlic slivers, and cook gently until light brown. Add half the basil leaves and the tomatoes, and cook, stirring over a fierce heat, until the tomatoes break up and reduce to a thick sauce. This should take about 15 minutes, if the tomatoes are ripe. If the tomatoes are unripe, they will be less juicy, so add some of the reserved tomato juices.

In another large, heavy saucepan, fry the chopped garlic in the remaining olive oil until light brown, then add the mussels and a few basil leaves and the remaining tomato juice, about 750 ml (1.1/4 pints). Cover with a tight-fitting lid, shake and cook over a high heat until the mussels are open (discard any that remain closed). You may need to do this in batches; divide the other ingredients accordingly. Leave to cool and then remove all the mussels from their shells.

Add the mussels to the tomato sauce with the rest of the basil, and season with sea salt and black pepper.

To make the bruschetta, toast the bread on both sides, then rub with the garlic. Serve the soup in flat open dishes with the bruschetta and a generous amount of extra virgin olive oil.

Zuppa di Pesce alla Ligure
Ligurian Fish Stew

In the River Cafe we serve this soup as a main course. You may vary the recipe according to the fish you can find, but always include a red fish such as mullet, a dense white fish such as turbot or monkfish (keep the bones for stock), and shellfish such as scallops, mussels or vongole.

Serves 6

3 x 175-225 g (6-8 oz) red mullet, scaled and cleaned

500 g (18 oz) monkfish or turbot fillets, boned weight (ask for the bones for stock)

1.5 kg (3.1/4 lb) mussels

12 langoustines (optional)

6 scallops, removed from their shells

175 ml (6 fl oz) olive oil

150 ml (5 fl oz) dry white wine

2 fresh red chillies, seeded and chopped

1.2 litres (2 pints) Fish Stock (see page 55)

12 small new potatoes, preferably Roseval, peeled

sea salt and freshly ground black pepper

5 garlic cloves, peeled and cut into slivers

4 fennel bulbs, sliced (keep the green leaves and stalks for stock)

25 g (1 oz) fennel seeds

1 x 800 g (1.3/4 lb) tin peeled plum tomatoes, drained of most of their juices, sieved

Crostini

6 slices ciabatta bread, cut at an angle

1 garlic clove, peeled and halved

1 bunch flat-leaf parsley (keep stalks for stock), chopped

Fillet the red mullet, and cut each fillet into four. Cut the monkfish or turbot into similar sized pieces.

Clean the mussels as described in the recipe on page 15, and put into a large saucepan with a tight-fitting lid, along with 120 ml (4 fl oz) of the olive oil, the white wine and half the chilli. Cover and steam over a high heat, shaking, until all the shells open, about 3-5 minutes. Discard any that remain closed. When cool, remove half the mussels from their shells, and strain the juices into the fish stock.

Bring the fish stock to the boil, and add the langoustines if using. Poach for 2 minutes, then remove and cool.

Boil the potatoes in salted water until nearly done. Drain and cool.

To make the tomato soup base, heat the remaining olive oil in a large, heavy-bottomed saucepan and fry the garlic, the remaining chilli, fennel and fennel seeds for a few minutes, then add the tomatoes, and cook over a gentle heat for about 45 minutes until thick and smooth. Be careful not to let it stick. Season to taste with salt and pepper, and add more chilli if you like.

Add half the fish stock to this sauce and bring to the boil. Now add the mullet, monkfish or turbot and scallops to the soup and bring back to the boil. Remove from the heat and add the cooked potatoes, mussels (shelled and unshelled), and langoustines. Divide between the bowls, making sure each person has some of each variety of fish.

To make the crostini, toast the bread on both sides and rub with the garlic. Put one crostini on top of each serving of soup, sprinkle with the chopped parsley and dribble extra virgin olive oil on top.

Zuppa Prosciutto e Piselli
Pea and Prosciutto Soup

Large fresh peas have a distinctive floury texture which is perfect for this soup. It is cooked slowly with the hock or tough end from a prosciutto.

Serves 6

2 kg (4.1/2 lb) peas, shelled (keep pods for the stock)

250 g (9 oz) prosciutto hock

1 head celery, trimmed and coarsely chopped

2 red onions, peeled

1 bunch fresh mint

2 carrots, peeled and coarsely chopped

2 tablespoons olive oil

50 g (2 oz) butter

sea salt and freshly ground black pepper

extra virgin olive oil or crème fraîche

Parmesan, freshly grated

To make the stock, gently simmer the prosciutto hock with the celery, one of the onions cut in half, the stalks of the mint, the carrots, pea pods and water to cover by 2.5 cm (1 in). This will take 1-1.1/2 hours.

Chop the remaining onion finely.

In a large, heavy saucepan, fry the chopped onion gently in the olive oil and the butter until light brown. Add half the mint leaves and the peas and stir together for a minute or two, then add enough of the strained stock to just cover the peas. Turn the heat to very low and simmer until the peas are soft, about 30-45 minutes, topping up with stock when necessary.

Remove the prosciutto hock from the stock and break the softest parts into pieces. Put in a processor with some stock and pulse briefly until a coarse purée.

When the peas are cooked remove half from the pan and pulse or chop in the blender with the stock they cooked in. Return to the pan and stir in along with the prosciutto purée. Chop the remainder of the mint leaves and add to the soup. Season if necessary.

Serve with extra virgin olive oil and Parmesan. Alternatively, you could serve it with crème fraîche and Parmesan.

Zuppa Estiva di Piselli
Summer Pea Soup

Young freshly picked peas are one of the most special early summer vegetables. This soup
celebrates that flavour.

Serves 6

1 kg (2.1/4 lb) fresh peas, shelled

1 tablespoon olive oil

25 g (1 oz) butter

1 medium red onion, peeled and finely chopped

1 garlic clove, peeled and very finely chopped

1 bunch fresh mint leaves, chopped

500 ml (17 fl oz) Chicken Stock (see page 54)

sea salt and freshly ground black pepper

50 g (2 oz) Parmesan, freshly grated

extra virgin olive oil

Melt the oil and butter together in a large saucepan, and fry the onion and garlic over a very gentle heat until soft but not brown, about 15 minutes. Add about three-quarters of the mint, the peas and the stock. Cook, covered, until the peas are tender, about 5 minutes.

Put half the mixture into a food processor and pulse until you have a coarse purée. Return to the pan and season. Add the remaining mint.

Serve sprinkled with Parmesan, and extra virgin olive oil.

Zuppa di Zucchine
Zucchini Soup

We use ridged zucchini that Adrian Baron grows for us in his walled garden in Suffolk. The flavour of this Italian variety is so good that we make it with water instead of chicken stock.

Serves 6

1 kg (2.1/4 lb) medium zucchini, trimmed

25 ml (1 fl oz) olive oil

2 garlic cloves, peeled and chopped

sea salt and freshly ground black pepper

500 ml (17 fl oz) Chicken Stock (see page 54) or water

140 ml (4.1/2 fl oz) double cream

1 small bunch basil, chopped

1 small bunch flat-leaf parsley, chopped

120 g (4.1/2 oz) Parmesan, freshly grated

Crostini

6 slices ciabatta bread, cut at an angle

115 g (4 oz) black olives, stoned and chopped

1 large fresh red chilli, seeded

extra virgin olive oil

Cut the zucchini lengthwise into quarters, then into 2.5 cm (1 in) pieces. Heat the oil in a heavy saucepan and cook the garlic and zucchini slowly for approximately 25 minutes until the zucchini are brown and very soft. Add salt, pepper and the stock, and simmer for another few minutes. Remove from the stove.

Put three-quarters of the zucchini in a food processor and purée. Return to the pan, and add the cream, basil, parsley and Parmesan.

To make the crostini, toast the bread on both sides. Mix the olives and chilli with some extra virgin olive oil and spread thickly on the crostini. Serve at the side of the plate.

Zuppa di Zucca
Pumpkin Soup

There are many varieties of pumpkin and squash. We use the ones that
have a deep orange flesh and that are moist when cut.

Serves 6

1.5 kg (3.1/4 lb) pumpkin, peeled, seeded and diced into 5 cm

(2 in) cubes

150 g (5 oz) new potatoes, peeled and cubed as above (preferably

yellow Charlotte or Roseval)

3 tablespoons olive oil

50 g (2 oz) butter

2 small red onions, peeled and finely chopped

2 garlic cloves, peeled and cut into slivers

4 large sprigs fresh marjoram

1-2 dried chillies

sea salt and freshly ground black pepper

1 litre (1.3/4 pints) Chicken Stock (see page 54)

Crostini

Parmesan, freshly grated

extra virgin olive oil

6 slices ciabatta bread

2 garlic cloves, peeled and halved

Heat the oil and butter in a large heavy saucepan and gently fry the onion until soft. Stir in the garlic and marjoram leaves, the pumpkin and potato, and continue to cook for a minute. Season with the chilli, salt and pepper. Add enough stock to just cover the pumpkin, turn down the heat, and simmer until the pumpkin is tender, about 20-25 minutes. You may need to add more stock.

Strain about a third of the stock from the pumpkin and set aside. Put the remainder in a food processor and pulse; The mixture should be very thick. Return this to the saucepan and add the stock you removed. Check for seasoning. This is a very thick soup.

Serve with Parmesan, new peppery olive oil and crostini made from toasted ciabatta rubbed with garlic and dipped into extra virgin olive oil.

Variation

Add 150 g (5 oz) cooked cannellini beans (see page 170) when you add the pumpkin. Reserve some whole ones to add to the final purée.

Zuppa di Acetosa e Lenticchie
Lentil and Sorrel Soup

Serves 6

250 g (9 oz) Puy lentils

2 garlic cloves, 1 unpeeled

50 g (2 oz) butter

2 tablespoons olive oil

1 small red onion, peeled and finely chopped

1 kg (2.1/4 lb) sorrel, stems removed

600 ml (1 pint) chicken stock (see page 54), hot

   sea salt and freshly ground black pepper

300 g (10 oz) young spinach leaves, stems removed

150 ml (5 fl oz) crème fraîche

75 g (3 oz) Parmesan

Put the lentils with an unpeeled clove of garlic in a saucepan with cold water to cover. Bring to the boil and simmer for about 25 minutes or until tender.

Melt the butter and olive oil in a large saucepan. Cook the onions and the remaining, peeled garlic clove until soft. Add half the sorrel and cook for a minute until the sorrel wilts. Stir in 3/4 of the lentils and the chicken stock. Season.

Transfer half the contents to a food processor, add the uncooked sorrel and spinach and pulse. Return to the saucepan and add the remaining lentils and chicken stock, then heat. Serve with crème fraîche and Parmesan.

Pappa al Pomodoro

This may be our favourite soup, especially in late summer when tomatoes and basil are at their best. It's important to use open-textured white bread made with olive oil, such as pugliese.

Serves 10

4 kg (9 lb) ripe sweet tomatoes, skinned and seeded, or

2 kg (4.1/2 lb) tinned plum tomatoes, drained of most of their juices

4 garlic cloves, peeled and cut into slivers

175 ml (6 fl oz) olive oil

sea salt and freshly ground black pepper

4 loaves stale pugliese bread

1 large bunch basil

extra virgin olive oil

Put the garlic and the olive oil into a heavy saucepan and cook gently for a few minutes. Just before the garlic turns brown, add the tomatoes. Simmer for 30 minutes, stirring occasionally, until the tomatoes become concentrated. Season with salt and pepper, then add 600 ml (1 pint) water and bring to the boil.

Cut most of the crust off the bread and break or cut into large chunks. Put the bread into the tomato mixture and stir until the bread absorbs the liquid, adding more boiling water if it is too thick. Remove from the heat and allow to cool slightly. If the basil leaves are large, tear into pieces. Stir into the soup with 120-175 ml (4-6 fl oz) of the extra virgin olive oil. Let sit before serving to allow the bread to absorb the flavour of the basil and oil. Add more of the extra virgin olive oil to each bowl.

Ribollita

Cavolo nero is essential for an authentic ribollita. Robust greens such as Swiss chard, the dark green outer leaves of Savoy cabbage, kale, broccoli or rape may be substituted.

Serves 10

250 g (9 oz) cannellini or borlotti beans, cooked (see page 170)

1 large bunch flat-leaf parsley, chopped

4 garlic cloves, peeled and chopped

2 whole heads celery, chopped

450 g (1 lb) carrots, peeled and chopped

4 medium red onions, peeled and chopped

4 tablespoons olive oil

1 x 800 g (1.3/4 lb) tin peeled plum tomatoes, drained of their juices

2 kg (4.1/2 lb) cavolo nero, stalks removed, leaves coarsely chopped

2 loaves stale ciabatta bread, crusts removed, sliced or torn

sea salt and freshly ground black pepper

extra virgin olive oil

In a large saucepan fry the parsley leaves, garlic, celery, carrot and onion in the oil for about 30 minutes until the flavours combine. Add the tomatoes and continue to cook on a gentle heat for a further 30 minutes, then add the cavolo nero and half the cannellini beans with enough of their liquid to cover. Simmer for 30 minutes.

In a food processor, purée the remaining beans and return to the soup with just enough boiling water to make the soup liquid. Add the bread, a generous amount of extra virgin olive oil, and season with salt and pepper. As exact amounts are not possible, you must balance the amount of liquid to bread so that the soup is very thick.

Minestrone Invernale
Winter Minestrone

The interesting texture and bright green colour of this minestrone is achieved by adding half the greens just before serving.

Serves 10

4 tablespoons olive oil

5 medium carrots, roughly chopped

3 medium red onions, peeled and coarsely chopped

2 heads celery, coarsely chopped, keeping the leaves

2 heads garlic, cloves peeled

2 kg (4.1/2 lb) Swiss chard, leaves shredded and stalks roughly chopped

1 small bunch parsley, finely chopped

1 x 800 g (1.3/4 lb) tin peeled plum tomatoes, drained of most of their juices, roughly
  chopped

2 kg (4.1/2 lb) cavolo nero, stalks removed, leaves shredded

250 g (9 oz) cannellini beans, cooked (see page 170)

1 litre (1.3/4 pints) Chicken Stock (see page 54) or water

sea salt and freshly ground black pepper

a few sprigs of winter herbs such as thyme or sage, chopped

Parmesan, freshly grated

extra virgin olive oil

For the soffritto heat the olive oil in a large saucepan and slowly fry the carrot, onion and celery until soft and dark. This will take a long time. Add the garlic, chard stalks, and half the parsley, and continue to cook, stirring to prevent sticking. Add the tomatoes and cook for 10 minutes or until they have reduced.

Add half the Swiss chard leaves and half the cavolo nero, three-quarters of the cooked beans, and the boiling chicken stock or water. Bring to the boil, then reduce the heat and simmer for 30 minutes. Add more stock if needed, but resist the temptation to add too much; this should be a thick soup.

Add the remaining Swiss chard and cavolo nero to the soup and blanch briefly so that they are cooked but remain green and crisp as a contrast to the rest of the soup. Season with salt and pepper, preferably when slightly cooled.

Purée the remaining cannellini beans coarsely in a blender, with some of the cooking liquid. Add to the soup. This soup should be very green. Stir in the herbs and serve hot with Parmesan and extra virgin olive oil.

Minestrone Estivo
Summer Minestrone

The summer vegetables are briefly cooked, and basil, marjoram or mint are added at the end.

Serves 10

2 garlic cloves, peeled and chopped

1 small head celery, chopped

3 small red onions, peeled and chopped

4 tablespoons olive oil

900 g (2 lb) thin asparagus, trimmed and cut into 1 cm (1/2 in) pieces using only tips and

   tender parts

450 g (1 lb) young green beans, trimmed and chopped

450 g (1 lb) peas, shelled

900 g (2 lb) broad beans, shelled

sea salt and freshly ground black pepper

about 1 litre (1.3/4 pints) Chicken Stock (see page 54)

1/2 bunch basil, finely chopped (or marjoram or mint)

300 ml (10 fl oz) double cream

150 g (5 oz) Parmesan, freshly grated

120 ml (4 fl oz) pesto

In a heavy saucepan fry the garlic, celery and onion gently in the olive oil until soft, about 10 minutes.

Divide all the other vegetables between two bowls. Add half to the onion mixture and cook, stirring to coat with oil, for a further 10 minutes. Season to taste with salt and pepper. Cover with chicken stock and bring to the boil. Simmer for 30 minutes.

Add the remaining vegetables and cook for a further 5 minutes. Remove from the heat and add the herbs, cream, Parmesan and pesto. Stir, cool to room temperature, then serve.

Zuppa di Fagioli Cannellini
Cannellini Bean Soup

When the new season's oil and dried cannellini beans arrive in November, we like to make this simple, unusual and comforting soup.

Serves 6

250 g (9 oz) cannellini beans

2-3 garlic cloves, peeled and chopped

3 tablespoons olive oil

1 bunch flat-leaf parsley, leaves chopped

sea salt and freshly ground pepper

extra virgin olive oil

Soak and cook the beans as described on page 170. Drain, and reserve the liquid.

In a large saucepan, cook the garlic in the oil until soft but not brown. Add the parsley and cook for a second, then add the beans and stir.

Put three-quarters of the mixture into a food processor with some of the liquid, and briefly pulse; you do not want a purée. Add more liquid if necessary, but it should be thick. Return to the saucepan and season with salt and pepper. If too thick, add more cooking liquid. Serve with a generous amount of extra virgin olive oil.

Variations *Escarole:* discard outer tough leaves of 2 medium heads. Wash the inside leaves but do not dry. Heat about 3 tablespoons olive oil in a frying pan and 'cook' the escarole briefly. Chop coarsely and add to the soup.

Cavolo nero or Swiss chard: use the Braised Cavolo Nero recipe on page 184. Chop coarsely and add to the soup.

Tomato and rosemary: peel and seed 1 kg (2.1/4 lb) fresh plum tomatoes. Chop coarsely and cook for 2 minutes in 2 tablespoons olive oil with 3 sprigs finely chopped fresh rosemary and 2-3 chopped garlic cloves. Add to the soup.

Porcini: soak 50 g (2 oz) dried porcini mushrooms, drain, cook, and add to the soup.

Zuppa di Fave Secche
Dried Broad Bean Soup

Dried broad beans have a totally different flavour and texture from fresh ones. In fact they taste soft and nutty, rather like chestnuts.

Serves 6-8

250 g (9 oz) dried broad beans, soaked and cooked (see page 170)

1 kg (2.1/4 lb) Swiss chard with stalks

3 garlic cloves, peeled and chopped

3 tablespoons olive oil

sea salt and freshly ground black pepper

extra virgin olive oil

Cook the beans as described on page 170, retaining their cooking water.

Remove the leaves from the chard stalks and shred them. Cut the upper part of the stalks into matchsticks. Blanch the stalks first in boiling salted water until tender – 5 minutes or so – then briefly blanch the leaves.

In a large saucepan, gently fry the garlic cloves in the olive oil until light brown. Add the blanched chard stalks and, after a minute, the blanched leaves. Stir to coat the chard with oil, then add half the cooked beans along with about a cupful of their cooking water. Cook for a further 5 minutes, no longer.

In a processor or blender, briefly pulse-chop the chard and bean mixture – the beans should be broken, not puréed. Add extra water from the cooked beans if necessary, but remember that the soup should be thick.

Return the mixture to the saucepan and add the remaining whole beans. Season with salt and pepper. Serve at room temperature with a generous amount of olive oil.

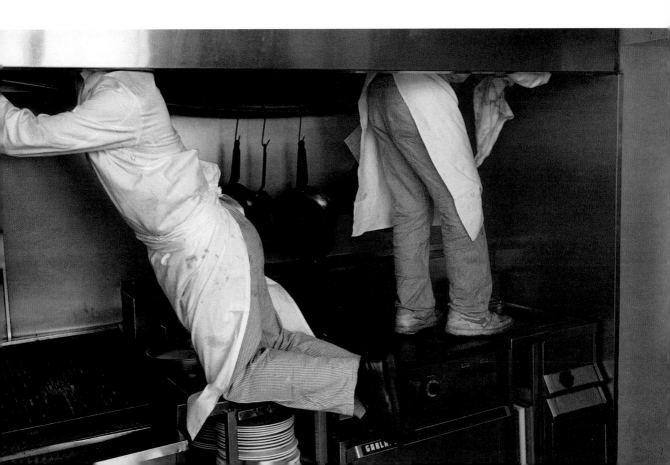

Pasta e Fagioli
Pasta and Bean Soup

Serves 10

250 g (9 oz) borlotti beans, soaked and cooked (see page 170)

4 tablespoons olive oil

3 red onions, peeled and finely chopped

1 head celery, including the leaves, chopped

4 garlic cloves, peeled and chopped

3 dried chillies, crumbled

1 bunch fresh rosemary, leaves finely chopped or pounded

200 g (7 oz) pancetta or prosciutto ends, cut into matchsticks

1 x 800 g (1.3/4 lb) tin peeled plum tomatoes

250 g (9 oz) penne rigate

sea salt and freshly ground black pepper

To serve

extra virgin olive oil

green chicory or dandelion leaves, chopped

Parmesan, freshly grated

Cook the beans as described on page 170, then leave to rest in their cooking water.

In a large heavy saucepan heat the oil and fry the onion and celery together over a medium heat. When the onion is soft but not brown, add the garlic, chilli, rosemary and pancetta or prosciutto, and continue to fry, stirring. The pancetta should become almost crisp. Add the tomatoes with their juices, breaking them up with a spoon, and continue to cook, reducing the liquid, for approximately 20 minutes.

In a blender, purée half the cooked beans with a little of their cooking water, then return to the saucepan with the remaining whole beans. Add a little more of the cooking liquid if the soup seems too thick.

In a separate pan cook the penne in boiling salted water until just al dente, drain and stir into the soup. Check for seasoning.

Serve with a generous helping of new season's extra virgin olive oil , the chopped leaves and grated Parmesan.

Zuppa di Mammole e Tompinambur
Globe and Jerusalem Artichoke Soup

Serves 10

8 large globe artichokes

1.5 kg (3.1/4 lb) Jerusalem artichokes, peeled

4 tablespoons olive oil

50 g (2 oz) butter

2 red onions, peeled and chopped

2 garlic cloves, peeled and chopped

2 dried chillies, crumbled

1 sprig fresh thyme

1.5 litres (2.1/2 pints) Chicken Stock (see page 54)

sea salt and freshly ground black pepper

Crostini

10 slices ciabatta bread, cut at an angle

2 garlic cloves, peeled and halved

10 sun-dried tomatoes, chopped

extra virgin olive oil

150 g (5 oz) Parmesan, freshly grated

Prepare the globe artichokes by removing the tough outer leaves, then cut off the tops of the leaves. Pare the stalks down to the paler tender part. Slice the artichokes into eighths. Remove the inner choke, which will be prickly and indigestible.

Cut each Jerusalem artichoke into small pieces roughly the same size as the pieces of globe.

Heat the olive oil and the butter in a heavy saucepan and fry the onion gently until light brown. Add the garlic and the prepared artichokes. Fry together to combine for 5-10 minutes. Add the chilli and thyme.

Heat the stock, season it well, and add just enough to cover the artichokes. Simmer, covered, until they are tender, usually about 15 minutes.

In a blender briefly pulse to chop the soup, but not to a purée. Return to the saucepan and add a little more stock. The soup should be thick but not stiff. Season.

To make the crostini, toast the ciabatta on both sides and rub with the raw garlic. Spread the chopped sun-dried tomatoes on each slice of toast.

Serve the soup with the crostini placed on top. Pour over some extra virgin olive oil, then sprinkle with Parmesan.

Zuppa dei Poveri

This soup is perfect for purple sprouting broccoli or cavolo nero. It is very simple to make, but it is essential to use your own stock.

Serves 10

2 kg (4.1/2 lb) purple sprouting broccoli

sea salt and freshly ground black pepper

10 slices ciabatta bread, cut at an angle

4 garlic cloves, peeled and halved

2 litres (3.1/2 pints) Chicken or Veal Stock (see pages 54 and 55)

Parmesan, freshly grated

Strip the tough stalks and tough outer leaves from the broccoli so that you are left with the spears and tender leaves. Blanch in boiling salted water. When the water comes back to the boil, remove the broccoli and drain.

To make the crostini, toast the ciabatta slices on both sides and rub with the garlic.

Bring the stock to the boil, season generously, and add the blanched broccoli spears. Cook for 2 minutes only.

In each soup bowl place a ladle of stock and broccoli spears. Sprinkle with Parmesan. Place the crostini on top and cover with a second ladle of stock and broccoli. Serve with more grated Parmesan on top.

Zuppa d'Aosta

A substantial baked soup from the mountainous north of Italy, with layers of cabbage, bread, mountain cheese, anchovies and Parmesan.

Serves 10

2 large Savoy cabbages

sea salt and freshly ground black pepper

2 loaves ciabatta bread

1 large garlic clove, peeled and halved

300 g (10 oz) salted anchovies

200 g (7 oz) Fontina cheese

2 litres (3.1/2 pints) Chicken Stock (see page 54)

100 g (4 oz) Parmesan, freshly grated

You will need a casserole or saucepan that can be put in the oven. Preheat the oven to moderate, 180°C/350°F/Gas 4.

Remove the leaves from the cabbage heads one by one, and cut out the thick stems from each leaf, keeping the leaves whole. Only use the leaves that are either dark or bright green. Blanch these in boiling salted water for 1 minute, then drain well.

Slice the ciabatta loaves in half lengthwise and cut off the tough exterior crusts. Toast each half on both sides and rub with the garlic.

Fillet the anchovies and wash off the salt. Dry well. Slice the Fontina into slivers. Bring the stock to the boil and season it.

In your casserole or pan make a first layer of cabbage leaves and season with salt and pepper. Place 3 or 4 anchovy fillets on top, then a layer of Fontina followed by half of the toasted ciabatta. Sprinkle over the Parmesan and add stock to cover this layer. Make a second layer in the same way, using up the remaining bread. Three layers are the ideal, but the shape of your pot will dictate the number you have. Your final layer should consist of cabbage, anchovies, Fontina and stock to cover. Try not to fill the pot to the top, as the soup level will rise as the ciabatta toast expands.

Bake in the preheated oven for 20-30 minutes. When ready, it should have a good cheese crust on the top.

Brodo di Pollo
Chicken Stock

Makes 2 litres (3.1/2 pints)

2 chicken carcasses, roasted or raw,

   plus giblets

1 red onion, peeled and halved

2 medium carrots, peeled

4 celery stalks

2 garlic cloves, peeled

a few flat-leaf parsley stalks

5 black peppercorns

3 bay leaves or thyme sprigs

sea salt

Put all the ingredients, except the sea salt, into a large saucepan, cover with 2.3-5 litres (4.1/4-5.1/4 pints) cold water, and bring to the boil, skimming off the scum as it comes to the surface. Lower the heat and simmer very gently for 1.1/2 hours.

Strain, season with salt, and leave to cool. If not using immediately keep in a refrigerator for up to two days.

Brodo di Vitello
Veal Stock

Makes 2 litres (3.1/2 pints)

3 veal shin or knuckle bones

1 red onion, peeled and halved

2 medium carrots, peeled

4 celery stalks

2 garlic cloves, peeled

a few flat-leaf parsley stalks

5 black peppercorns

3 bay leaves or thyme sprigs

sea salt

Roast the veal bones for 40 minutes in an oven preheated to 180°C/350°F/Gas 4. Deglaze the pan with a little boiling water, scraping up any caramelised juices from the bottom.

Put the bones, the roasting juices and all the other ingredients except the salt into a large pan, cover with 2.5-3 litres (4.1/4-5.1/4 pints) cold water, and bring to the boil, skimming off the scum as it comes to the surface. Lower the heat and simmer very gently for up to but no more than 2 hours.

Strain, season with salt, and leave to cool. If not using immediately, keep in a refrigerator for up to two days.

Note For a light veal stock it is not necessary to roast the bones first.

Brodo di Pesce
Fish Stock

The best fish stock is made from the bones of a turbot.

Makes 2 litres (3.1/2 pints)

bones of 1 large turbot including the
    head, halibut or monkfish

2 red onions, peeled and cut in
    quarters lengthways

2 carrots, sliced

4 celery stalks

a few flat-leaf parsley stalks

6 white or black peppercorns

2 bay leaves

1 fennel bulb, untrimmed, cut in half

Put the ingredients into a large saucepan, cover with about 2 litres (3.1/2 pints) cold water, and bring to the boil, skimming off the scum as it comes to the surface. Lower the heat and simmer gently for 15 minutes; in order to achieve a fresh-tasting stock, do not be tempted to do so for longer than this.

Strain and use immediately.

Past
Riso

a &
tto
2

An Italian cook will look first in the cupboard to see what pasta there is and depending on the type of pasta, will then decide what sauce to make. Our Italian friends would not dream of serving a carbonara sauce with any other pasta than penne, or a vongole with anything other than spaghetti. There is a logic to these rules: creamy thick sauces need the support of the sturdier, thicker shapes of pens, tubes, and shells; oil-based sauces such as those made with crab, vongole or anchovies are best with long thin pasta – spaghetti, linguine or bucatini.

At the River Cafe our choice of pasta dishes is seasonal, with comforting, robust recipes in the winter and fresher ones in the summer. The time of day also influences the type of pasta we cook, with more sturdy sauces and dried pasta at lunch and the more refined sauces with fresh pasta in the evening.

The basic method for making risotto rarely varies. It is essential to know the steps, but only after practice, and, more importantly, knowing what you are aiming for, is it possible to make a perfect risotto. Rhythm, timing, and, above all, patience are as important as the ingredients that you use.

Although this is a restaurant cookbook, risotto is most successfully made at home when you have plenty of time, as slow cooking is the only way to achieve the correct balance of rice and liquid. The stages of adding ingredients to the risotto are part of the rhythm and preparation and depend on the ingredients you are using. There is no strict measure of stock, as it will vary according to the type of rice and intensity of heat.

The risotto is ready when the grain is al dente and the mixture moist and creamy. Just before taking the risotto of the heat we like to add a small amount of dry vermouth to add a distinctive taste.

Pasta all' Uovo
Fresh Pasta

This pasta dough is made in a food processor. It is important to use free-range eggs and Italian pasta flour labelled Tipo 'OO'.

Makes approximately 1 kg (2.1/4 lb)

700 g (a good 1.1/2 lb) pasta flour or plain white flour

1/2 teaspoon sea salt

4 whole eggs (5 if they are small)

9 egg yolks (10 if the eggs are small)

about 100 g (4 oz) medium semolina flour

Put the flour and salt in a processor and add the eggs and egg yolks. Pulse-blend until the pasta begins to come together into a loose ball of dough.

Knead the pasta dough on a flat surface, lightly dusted with the semolina and a little extra flour, until the mixture is smooth, about 3 minutes. If the dough is very stiff and difficult to knead, you may have to put it back in the processor and blend in another whole egg.

Cut the dough into eight equal-sized pieces and briefly knead them into individual balls. Wrap each ball in cling film and allow to rest in a refrigerator for at least 20 minutes, and up to 2 hours.

To prepare your dough for cutting into either tagliatelle or ravioli, put it through a pasta machine, following the manufacturer's instructions. We put each ball through at the thickest setting ten

times, folding the sheet into three each time to get a short thick strip, and then turn it by a quarter, and put it through the machine again. After ten such folds the pasta will feel silky. Only then reduce the machine setting gradually down to the thinness required. For tagliatelle, you will need 2, for the rotolo, 1.5, for ravioli, a very thin setting of 0.5. These are the settings for our large commercial machine, but all machines are different.

If rolling by hand, you will have to hand-knead and hand-roll the dough the equivalent of ten times through the machine. This needs to be done in a cool place so that the pasta does not dry.

Penne alla Carbonara

For us the two most important ingredients are excellent free-range eggs, and pancetta stesa.

Serves 6

200 g (7 oz) pancetta, cut into matchsticks

1 tablespoon olive oil

sea salt and freshly ground black pepper

6 egg yolks

120 ml (4 fl oz) double cream

150 g (5 oz) Parmesan, freshly grated

250 g (9 oz) penne rigate

In a large pan fry the pancetta in the olive oil slowly, so that it releases its own fat before becoming crisp. Add some black pepper.

Beat the egg yolks with the cream and season with salt and pepper. Add half the Parmesan.

Meanwhile, cook the penne in a generous amount of boiling salted water, then drain thoroughly. Combine immediately with the hot pancetta and the oil, and then pour in the cream mixture. Stir to coat each pasta piece; the heat from the pasta will cook the egg slightly. Finally add the remaining Parmesan and serve.

Variation

Asparagus: instead of the pancetta, cut 675 g (1.1/2 lb) blanched asparagus into short pieces and fry briefly in oil with a handful of basil leaves. Add to the pasta before combining with the egg sauce.

Rotolo di Spinaci

Our version of this classic is unusually light: ricotta and spinach thinly wrapped in pasta and poached.

Serves 4-6

1/2 quantity Fresh Pasta (see page 60)

semolina flour for dusting

For the filling

20 g (3/4 oz) butter

1/2 red onion, peeled and finely chopped

1 handful fresh marjoram

800 g (1.3/4 lb) fresh spinach, washed, blanched and chopped

sea salt and freshly ground black pepper

65 g (2.1/2 oz) dried porcini mushrooms, reconstituted (see page 312)

1.1/2 tablespoons olive oil

2 garlic cloves, peeled and chopped

225 g (8 oz) field mushrooms, coarsely sliced

about 350 g (12 oz) fresh ricotta cheese

65 g (2.1/2 oz) Parmesan, freshly grated

freshly grated nutmeg

To serve

extra grated Parmesan

Sage Butter (see page 68)

To make the filling, heat the butter in a pan and fry the onion until soft, then add the marjoram and spinach. Stir to combine the flavours, season, then cool.

Drain the porcini, reserving the soaking liquid. Wash to remove grit. Heat the oil in a pan, and fry the garlic gently for a few minutes. Add the field mushrooms, stirring all the time, and cook fast for 5 minutes. Add the porcini and continue to fry gently for 20 minutes, adding a little of the porcini liquid from time to time to make the mushrooms moist, not wet. Season and leave to cool. When cold, chop roughly.

Put the ricotta in a large bowl, mix lightly with a fork to break it up, then add the spinach mixture, Parmesan and a generous amount of nutmeg. Add salt and pepper if necessary. Set aside.

Roll the pasta out by hand on a work surface, dusted with semolina flour, to a large sheet, as thin as possible; it does not matter if there are a few holes or tears. Cut the edges to straighten. You should have a piece of about 30 cm (1 ft) square.

If you have a pasta machine, roll out two strips and join to make a square by brushing the edges with water to seal.

Spoon the mushroom mixture along the edge of the pasta nearest to you, in a line about 3 cm (1.1/2 in) wide. Cover the rest of the pasta with the spinach and ricotta mixture to a thickness of about 5 mm - 1 cm (1/4 - 1/2 in). Now, starting with the mushroom edge, gently roll up the pasta into a large sausage, working away from you.

Place the pasta roll on a large clean tea towel and wrap in the cloth as tightly as you can. Secure with string to hold the roll in shape.

Fill a fish kettle with water and bring to the boil. Add salt and the pasta roll, cover and simmer for 18-20 minutes, according to the thickness of the roll. We usually make rolls of 6-7 cm (2.1/2 - 2.3/4 in) in diameter.

Unwrap the pasta roll, place on a board and cut into 1 cm (1/2 in) slices. Serve four to six slices per person, with extra grated Parmesan and some sage butter.

Ravioli di Magro
Ravioli with Swiss Chard and Pancetta

The blended flavours of Swiss chard and pancetta make an unusual filling for ravioli.

Serves 10

1 quantity Fresh Pasta (see page 60)

semolina flour for dusting

For the filling

1 kg (2.1/4 lb) Swiss chard

sea salt and freshly ground black pepper

100 g (4 oz) butter

2 small red onions, peeled and finely chopped

250 g (9 oz) pancetta stesa, cut into matchsticks

250 g (9 oz) fresh ricotta cheese

1/2 nutmeg, freshly grated

100 g (4 oz) Parmesan, freshly grated

For the sage butter

225 g (8 oz) unsalted butter

1 bunch sage, leaves separated from the stalks

Cut the leaves of the Swiss chard from their stalks, and blanch, drain and roughly chop. Finely chop about 150 g (5 oz) of the stalks (the whiter the stalk, the more tender), and blanch them separately in boiling salted water.

Heat the butter in a heavy saucepan and gently fry the onion until soft and beginning to colour. Add the blanched stalks and the pancetta and cook together for a few minutes – just long enough for the pancetta to become translucent, but not crisp. The pancetta flavour should blend together with the onion and stalks. Season, then add the chard leaves and cook for a few minutes. Remove from the heat and cool.

In a large bowl break up the ricotta using a fork. Season with nutmeg, sea salt and black pepper. Add half the cooled chard mixture and stir together lightly. Add the Parmesan and the remainder of the chard, and fold together. The mixture should not be at all wet; if it seems so, add a little extra Parmesan. Taste for seasoning, and ensure that the mixture is completely cold before making the ravioli.

Divide the pasta into small amounts the size of a large egg. Using a pasta machine roll them out into long strips (one at a time to prevent drying) as thin as possible. (See page 60.) Cut in half if too long.

Put teaspoons of filling about 6 cm (2.1/4 in) apart on the sheet, in the centre of the half nearest you, so that you can fold the other half over to make a 'parcel'. Brush around the fillings with a pastry brush dipped in water before folding, so that the envelopes you are making will seal properly. Using a pasta cutter, seal each envelope by cutting on three sides (the fourth is the fold). Dust a large plate or tray with semolina flour and carefully place the ravioli on it, making sure that they do not touch. You should have about fifty.

To make the sage butter, heat the butter gently so that it separates. Pour out the clarified butter, return to the heat and, when very hot, add the sage for a second or two. Remove from the heat and allow to cool.

Bring a large pan of salted water to the boil, and put in the ravioli. Lower heat to simmer: the ravioli will pop up to the surface of the water after 30 seconds, but according to how thin you managed to roll the pasta, they will take up to 2 minutes to cook. Test on the join of the envelope where the pasta is thickest.

Serve the ravioli on warm plates with 3-4 sage leaves, a little of the melted butter and some extra Parmesan.

Ravioli di Zucca e Mascarpone
Ravioli with Pumpkin

Make these ravioli as in the previous recipe, and serve with the same sage butter, or with Parmesan and white truffle oil.

Serves 10

1 quantity Fresh Pasta (see page 60)

semolina flour for dusting

For the filling

2 kg (4.1/2 lb) ripe, deep yellow pumpkin, whole or 1 large slice, skin on

2 tablespoons olive oil

sea salt and freshly ground black pepper

50 g (2 oz) butter

1 large red onion, peeled and finely chopped

2 garlic cloves, peeled and chopped

1 dried chilli, crumbled

1 bunch fresh marjoram

1/2 nutmeg, freshly grated

500 g (18 oz) mascarpone

150 g (5 oz) Parmesan, freshly grated

Preheat the oven to 220°C/425°F/Gas 7.

Remove the seeds and fibre from the centre of the pumpkin, and cut it into large chunks. Place on a baking tray brushed with olive oil, and season generously with salt and pepper. Bake in the preheated oven until soft, about 50 minutes. The pumpkin is ready when it has shrivelled and begun to brown at the edges. Remove from the oven, allow the pumpkin to cool, then scrape the soft flesh from the skins.

Heat the butter in a heavy pan and gently fry the onion until soft and beginning to colour. Add the garlic, chilli and marjoram, and fry just to blend the flavours with the onion. Add the pumpkin pulp, stir and cook for a few minutes longer to combine and, if the pumpkin is wet, to reduce any liquid. This mixture must be seasoned generously with salt, pepper and nutmeg. Place in a large bowl in the refrigerator to cool.

When absolutely cold, fold in the mascarpone and Parmesan.

Roll out the pasta as described in the previous recipe and make the ravioli. Cook as in the previous recipe.

Penne con Pomodoro e Aceto Balsamico
Penne with Tomato and Balsamic Vinegar

We use a ten-year-old balsamic vinegar to colour and flavour the penne. If
you don't, you may need an extra couple of tablespoons.

Serves 6

2 tablespoons olive oil

2 garlic cloves, peeled and cut into slivers

a handful of fresh basil

1 x 800 g (1.3/4 lb) tin peeled plum tomatoes

sea salt and freshly ground black pepper

250 g (9 oz) penne rigate

75 g (3 oz) butter, cut into pieces

4 tablespoons balsamic vinegar, 10 year old plus

120 g (4.1/2 oz) Pecorino cheese, freshly grated

Heat the oil in a large pan and gently fry the garlic slivers until light brown. Add a few
of the basil leaves and then the tomatoes. Stir and cook gently for 30-40 minutes,
until reduced to a thick sauce. Season with salt and pepper and add the remaining
basil.

Cook the penne in a generous amount of boiling salted water, drain thoroughly and
return to the saucepan with the butter. When this has melted, add the balsamic
vinegar and toss over a gentle heat for a few seconds until the penne are brown in
colour. Throw in a handful of the grated Pecorino, and finally stir in the tomato sauce.
Serve with more Pecorino.

Penne all' Amatriciana

The secret of a successful amatriciana is the initial infusion of the pancetta and onion.

Serves 6

250 g (9 oz) pancetta stesa, cut into matchsticks

2 tablespoons olive oil

2 dried chillies, crumbled

2 red onions, peeled and finely chopped

150 ml (5 fl oz) red wine

1 x 800 g (1.3/4 lb) tin peeled plum tomatoes, drained if very liquid

2 tablespoons rosemary

sea salt and freshly ground black pepper

250 g (9 oz) penne

100 g (4 oz) Parmesan, freshly grated

A handful of fresh oregano

Place the pancetta, oil and chillies in a large saucepan, heat and fry until the pancetta becomes crisp. Then add the onions and rosemary and continue to fry until they have also become light brown and crisp. Add the red wine – it will reduce almost immediately – then the tomatoes and season with the oregano and pepper. Bring to the boil, lower the heat and simmer for at least 45 minutes, until thick and almost dry. Check for seasoning.

Cook the penne in a generous amount of boiling salted water, then drain thoroughly. Add to the sauce, mix, and serve with Parmesan.

Penne con Melanzane
Penne with Aubergine

Serves 6

2 medium aubergines

sea salt and freshly ground black pepper

olive oil

3 garlic cloves, peeled and chopped

5 tablespoons finely chopped flat-leaf parsley

2 dried chillies, crumbled

1 x 800 g (1.3/4 lb) tin peeled plum tomatoes, or 1.3 kg (3 lb) fresh

   tomatoes, skinned, seeded and chopped

250 g (9 oz) penne rigate

150 g (5 oz) mozzarella di bufala, freshly grated

120 g (4.1/2 oz) Parmesan, freshly grated

Thinly slice the aubergines, sprinkle with salt and leave in a colander to drain of any bitter juices for 30 minutes. Rinse and dry.

While they are draining, heat 3 tablespoons olive oil in a large pan and add the garlic, parsley and chilli. Fry gently for almost 5 minutes. When the garlic has turned brown, add the tomatoes and cook for 20 minutes. This sauce has a more liquid consistency.

Heat 3 more tablespoons of the olive oil in a frying pan and add aubergine slices to cover the bottom. Fry on both sides until light brown and crisp. Drain well on kitchen paper. Repeat until all the aubergine is cooked.

Cook the penne in a generous amount of boiling salted water. Drain thoroughly, return to the pan and mix in the sauce, the aubergine and the grated cheeses. Serve immediately.

Penne con Sugo di Salsiccie alla Cloe
Penne with a Quick Sausage Sauce

Our Tuscan friends, Cloe and Adam gave us these two recipes. Hers takes 20 minutes, his 1.1/2 hours.

Serves 6

2 tablespoons olive oil

2 small red onions, peeled and chopped

5 Italian spiced, fresh pork sausages, meat removed from skins and crumbled

1.1/2 tablespoons chopped fresh rosemary

2 bay leaves

2 small dried chillies, crumbled

1 x 800 g (1.3/4 lb) tin peeled plum tomatoes, drained and chopped

sea salt and freshly ground black pepper

250 g (9 oz) penne rigate

150 ml (5 fl oz) double cream

120 g (4.1/2 oz) Parmesan, freshly grated

In a large saucepan, heat the oil and fry the onion until light brown. Add the crumbled sausage, the rosemary, bay leaves and chilli. Fry together over a high heat, stirring to mash the sausages. Remove all but 1 tablespoon of the fat, and continue to cook for 20 minutes. The sausagemeat should become brown and disintegrate. Add the tomatoes, stir and return to the boil. Remove from the stove.

Cook the penne in a generous amount of boiling salted water, then drain thoroughly.

Stir the cream into the sauce along with the drained penne and half the Parmesan. Serve with the remaining Parmesan.

Penne con Sugo di Salsiccie alla Adam
Penne with a Slow-Cooked Sausage Sauce

Serves 6

2 tablespoons olive oil

8 Italian spiced, fresh pork sausages, meat removed from skins and crumbled

2 small red onions, peeled and chopped

2 garlic cloves, peeled and chopped

2 small dried chillies, crumbled

2 bay leaves

1/3 bottle red wine (preferably Chianti or Sangiovese)

1 x 800 g (1.3/4 lb) tin peeled plum tomatoes, drained

1/2 nutmeg, freshly grated

sea salt and freshly ground black pepper

120 g (4.1/2 oz) Parmesan, freshly grated

150 ml (5 fl oz) double cream

250 g (9 oz) penne rigate

Heat the oil in a large pan, and fry the sausagemeat, stirring and breaking up the pieces. After the juice from the meat has evaporated and the fat begins to run, add the onion, garlic, chilli and bay leaves. Cook gently for almost 30 minutes until the onions are brown. Pour in the wine, increase the heat and cook until the wine evaporates. Now add the tomatoes, lower the heat, and simmer gently until you have a thick sauce, about 45-60 minutes. Season with nutmeg and salt (and pepper, if the sausages were not spicy), and add the Parmesan and cream.

Cook the penne in a generous amount of boiling salted water, then drain well. Add the penne to the sauce, combine and serve.

Pappardelle alla Lepre
Pappardelle with Hare

This Tuscan classic is the only fresh meat sauce we make at the River Cafe.

Serves 6

1 small hare, jointed into small pieces (legs and saddle divided into 4 pieces)

4 tablespoons olive oil

flour for dusting

sea salt and freshly ground black pepper

1 large onion, peeled and finely chopped

1 carrot, finely chopped

1 celery stalk, finely chopped

2 garlic cloves, peeled and finely chopped

1 x 400 g (14 oz) tin peeled plum tomatoes, drained of their juices

1/2 bottle red wine

3 cloves

1/2 cinnamon stick

250 g (9 oz) fresh pappardelle

3 tablespoons double cream

2 tablespoons freshly grated Parmesan

Heat half the olive oil in a heavy-bottomed pan. Dust the hare pieces in flour seasoned with salt and pepper, and then fry in the hot oil until evenly brown and well coloured. Remove from the pan and set aside. Pour the remaining oil into the pan, lower the heat, and soften the onion, carrot and celery until they start to caramelise, about 15 minutes.

Add the garlic and tomatoes and cook for a further 15 minutes. Simmer for 15 minutes. Pour in the red wine and allow to reduce for a further 10 minutes. Lower the heat to a gentle simmer and add salt, pepper, spices and the hare pieces. Cook gently for 1 hour, stirring occasionally.

After an hour the saddle pieces will be cooked, so remove and put to one side, leaving the legs to cook for a further 30 minutes. If the sauce seems dry, add a little boiling water, about 120 ml (4 fl oz).

Remove the meat from both the saddle and legs, keeping the two meats separate, and break into pieces.

Discard the cloves and cinnamon from the sauce. Put the sauce and leg meat through a food mill or into a liquidiser, and pulse until all the meat has been finely chopped (about a minute). Put in a saucepan with the cream and chopped saddle meat, heat through and check for seasoning.

Cook the pappardelle in a generous amount of boiling salted water. Drain thoroughly, combine with the sauce, and serve immediately with the Parmesan.

Penne con Pomodoro e Acciughe
Penne with Tomato and Anchovy Sauce

You must use salted anchovies from Greek, Spanish and Italian delicatessens. Small tins of anchovies soaked in oil are not suitable.

Serves 6

2 tablespoons olive oil

50 g (2 oz) butter

2 garlic cloves, peeled and sliced

10 salted anchovies, washed and dried

2 tablespoons fresh rosemary leaves, finely chopped

1 x 800 g (1.3/4 lb) tin peeled plum tomatoes

150 ml (5 fl oz) double cream

120 g (4.1/2 oz) Parmesan, freshly grated

250 g (9 oz) penne, rigatoni or conchiglie

sea salt

Melt the oil and butter together in a large pan, and fry the garlic gently until light brown. Add the anchovies and rosemary and then mash them into the oil, almost to a paste. The anchovies do not need to cook, they just melt; this only takes a few seconds.

Add the tomatoes to the paste and stir to break them up. Bring to the boil, then reduce the heat and simmer until the liquid has evaporated and the tomatoes have become a sauce, about 30-45 minutes. Finally, add the cream and bring to the boil stirring, then add most of the Parmesan.

Cook the pasta in a generous amount of boiling salted water, then drain thoroughly. Stir into the sauce, and serve with the remaining Parmesan.

Conchiglie al Cavolo Nero

Cavolo nero has a strong unique flavour. The cavolo nero should have had its first frost, which affects the texture and intensifies the flavour.

Serves 6

900 g (2 lb) cavolo nero

sea salt and freshly ground black pepper

300 ml (10 fl oz) double cream

7 garlic cloves, peeled

3 tablespoons extra virgin olive oil

2-3 dried chillies (depending on how hot you like the pasta), crumbled

150 g (5 oz) Parmesan, freshly grated

250 g (9 oz) conchiglie

Remove the tough central stalk from each leaf of cavolo nero, and cut each leaf into three or four pieces. Blanch in boiling salted water for a few minutes only, until tender and bright green. Drain and dry.

Put the double cream and 5 whole garlic cloves into a pan and simmer until the garlic is soft. Purée in a blender.

In a separate pan, heat the olive oil and fry the remaining garlic, cut into thin slices, and the chilli. When the garlic has coloured, add the blanched cavolo nero, stir and season. Pour in the cream and garlic purée, bring to the boil, and cook for 5 minutes until the cavolo nero is coated and the sauce has thickened. Add the Parmesan.

Cook the pasta in a generous amount of boiling salted water, then drain thoroughly. Add to the sauce and mix well.

Farfalle al Cavolo Nero con Olio Nuovo

The family Bonaccossi, who own the winery at the Medici Villa, Capezzana, gave us this recipe to go with the new season's olive oil.

Serves 6

1.1 kg (2.1/2 lb) cavolo nero leaves

sea salt and freshly ground black pepper

4 garlic cloves, peeled

250 ml (8 fl oz) extra virgin olive oil

250 g (9 oz) farfalle

Parmesan, freshly grated

Remove the stalks of the cavolo nero leaves, but keep the leaves whole. Blanch them in a generous amount of boiling salted water along with 2 garlic cloves for a few minutes only. Drain well. Put the blanched garlic and cavolo nero into the food processor and pulse-chop to a fairly coarse purée. In the last couple of seconds, pour into the processor about 75 ml (2.1/2 fl oz) of the oil. This makes a fairly liquid, dark green purée.

Crush the 2 remaining garlic cloves with 1 teaspoon sea salt. Stir into the purée along with a further 75 ml (2.1/2 fl oz) oil. Season to taste.

Cook the farfalle in a generous amount of boiling salted water, then drain thoroughly. Put the pasta into the sauce and stir until each piece is thickly coated. Pour in the remaining olive oil and serve with Parmesan.

Conchiglie al Pomodoro e Porcini Secchi

Serves 6

75 g (3 oz) dried porcini mushrooms, reconstituted (see page 312)

4 tablespoons olive oil

3 garlic cloves, peeled and sliced

1 tablespoon fresh thyme leaves

2 tablespoons flat-leaf parsley, finely chopped

1 dried chilli, crumbled

juice of 1 lemon

1 x 800 g (1.3/4 lb) tin peeled plum tomatoes, drained of their juices

120 ml (4 fl oz) double cream

120 g (4.1/2 oz) Parmesan, freshly grated

250 g (9 oz) conchiglie

sea salt and freshly ground black pepper

extra virgin olive oil

Heat the olive oil in a pan and fry the garlic gently for a few minutes with the thyme leaves, most of the parsley and the chilli. Add the porcini and cook for a few more minutes to combine the flavours. Add the porcini liquid a little at a time – it will be absorbed very quickly – and continue simmering until the porcini are tender, approximately 20 minutes. (The better quality porcini take much less time to cook.)

Add the lemon juice, then the tomatoes. Cook together gently until the tomatoes have thickened and become a sauce, about 30 minutes. Add the cream and reduce very briefly by boiling. Season, then remove from the heat and stir in half the Parmesan.

Cook the conchiglie in a generous amount of boiling salted water, then drain thoroughly. Add to the sauce with most of the remaining Parmesan and stir well. Serve sprinkled with the remaining parsley and Parmesan and a dribble of extra virgin olive oil.

Spaghetti al Limone

This recipe comes from Genoa which claims to have the most fragrant basil. If you can get lemons that have not been sprayed, grate a little of the zest and add to the sauce at the last minute.

Serves 6

250 g (9 oz) spaghetti

sea salt and freshly ground black pepper

juice of 3-4 lemons, the freshest possible

150 ml (5 fl oz) olive oil

150 g (5 oz) Parmesan, freshly grated

2 handfuls fresh basil, leaves finely chopped

Cook the spaghetti in a generous amount of boiling salted water, then drain thoroughly and return to the saucepan.

Meanwhile, beat the lemon juice with the olive oil, then stir in the Parmesan until thick and creamy. The Parmesan will melt into the mixture. Season, and add more or less lemon juice to taste.

Add the sauce to the spaghetti, and shake the pan so that each strand is coated with the cheese. Finally, stir in the chopped basil and, ideally, some grated lemon zest.

Spaghetti alle Vongole in Bianco
Spaghetti with Clams

Use the smallest clams. Vongole in Italy are about the size of a pound coin.

Serves 6

3 kg (6.1/2 lb) clams

100 ml (3.1/2 fl oz) olive oil

150 ml (5 fl oz) white wine

3 garlic cloves, peeled and sliced

3 small dried chilies, crumbled

250 g (9 oz) spaghetti or linguine

3 tablespoons chopped flat-leaf parsley

sea salt and freshly ground black pepper

Place the clams in a sink of cold water and wash thoroughly by scrubbing the shells with a coarse brush. Soak in clean water, changing the water until it is clear.

Heat one-third of the olive oil in a large saucepan with a lid. Add half the wine, 1 garlic clove and 1 chilli. Add half the clams, cover with a lid, and cook on a high heat until they open, shaking the pan constantly. When the shells are open, remove the clams to a large bowl, with their juices. Repeat with the remainder of the clams.

When all the clams have been cooked, chop the remaining garlic and chilli, and fry until light brown in the remaining oil. Add the clams and their juices, and remove immediately.

Cook the spaghetti or linguine in a generous amount of boiling salted water, then drain thoroughly. Place in the clam pan. Mix well to coat the pasta with the juices. Add the chopped parsley and black pepper.

Conchiglie con Broccoli

It is best to use the large pasta shells for this recipe. Use purple sprouting broccoli with its leaves or alternatively cime di rapa.

Serves 6

1.1 kg (2.1/2 lb) broccoli heads and leaves

sea salt and freshly ground black pepper

2 tablespoons olive oil

3 large garlic cloves, peeled and cut into fine slivers

2 small dried chillies, crumbled

100 g (4 oz) salted anchovies, prepared (see page 304)

50 g (2 oz) unsalted butter

150 ml (5 fl oz) double cream

250 g (9 oz) large conchiglie

120 g (4.1/2 oz) Parmesan, freshly grated

Cut the broccoli vertically into small pieces so that each has flower, stalk and leaf. Blanch very briefly in boiling salted water.

Heat the oil in a large heavy saucepan and fry the garlic gently until light brown. Add the chilli, the anchovies and butter. Mash the anchovies with the garlic using a wooden spoon; they should go creamy. Add the broccoli and the cream, bring to the boil, then simmer for 6 minutes or less. Larger heads will take longer to break up.

Mash or pulse-chop half of the broccoli sauce in a blender and then return to the pan with the other half of the sauce.

Cook the conchiglie in a generous amount of boiling salted water, then drain well and mix into the sauce. Season with salt and pepper and half the Parmesan. Serve sprinkled with the remaining Parmesan.

Tagliarini al Bosco
Tagliarini with Asparagus and Herbs

In Italy they use wild asparagus, hence 'al bosco'. We use young thin stalks.

Serves 6

675 g (1.1/2 lb) thin asparagus stalks, tough ends trimmed

sea salt and freshly ground black pepper

250 ml (8 fl oz) double cream

4 garlic cloves, peeled 3 whole, 1 chopped

2 tablespoons olive oil

50 g (2 oz) butter

4 tablespoons finely chopped fresh herb or mixed herbs (basil, mint, parsley, oregano)

250 g (9 oz) tagliarini or tagliatelle

120 g (4.1/2 oz) Parmesan, freshly grated

Cut the stalks into 2 cm (3/4 in) slices at an angle. Blanch the stalks in boiling salted water for 1 minute. Blanch the tips for seconds only. Drain well.

Bring the cream to the boil in a large saucepan with the whole garlic cloves and simmer until the cloves are soft. Remove from the heat, and discard the garlic.

Heat the oil and butter in a separate saucepan and fry the remaining garlic until light brown. Add the herbs and stalks, and cook briefly just to coat them in the butter and oil, then pour in the flavoured cream. Bring to the boil, reduce the heat, and simmer until the cream begins to thicken, about 6 minutes. Season.

Cook the pasta in a generous amount of boiling salted water, then drain thoroughly. Add to the sauce along with about half of the Parmesan and the asparagus tips. Serve with the remaining Parmesan.

Bucatini con Origano
Bucatini with Fresh and Dried Oregano

This recipe came from Il Vipore, a restaurant in the hills outside Lucca. It is the abundance of dried and fresh oregano that makes it so interesting.

Serves 6

2 large handfuls fresh oregano, very finely chopped

50 g (2 oz) dried oregano, crumbled

8 red cherry tomatoes, seeded and finely chopped

8 yellow cherry tomatoes, seeded and finely chopped

85 ml (3 fl oz) extra virgin olive oil

sea salt and freshly ground black pepper

250 g (9 oz) bucatini

Mix the fresh and dried oregano together.

Marinate the tomatoes with half of the olive oil, and some salt and pepper.

Cook the bucatini in a generous amount of boiling salted water, then drain thoroughly, and return to the pan. Toss with the oregano mixture and the remaining olive oil. Place a small amount of the tomato on top of each serving.

Spaghetti con Bottarga

This recipe comes from Sardinia where the best bottarga can be found.

Serves 6

250 g (9 oz) spaghetti or linguine

sea salt and freshly ground black pepper

3 tablespoons olive oil

2 garlic cloves, peeled and finely chopped

50 g (2 oz) flat-leaf parsley, very finely chopped

2 dried chillies, crumbled

300 g (10 oz) bottarga, coarsely grated

juice of 2 lemons

Cook the pasta in a generous amount of boiling salted water, then drain thoroughly and return to the saucepan.

Meanwhile, heat the olive oil in a separate saucepan and fry the garlic, parsley and chilli for a few seconds. Add to the drained pasta, then stir in most of the bottarga.

Serve immediately with the remaining bottarga on top, and a squeeze of lemon.

Linguine con Sardine

Serves 6

900 g (2 lb) fresh sardines

2 tablespoons olive oil

2 garlic cloves, peeled and finely sliced

2 small dried chillies, crumbled

2 tablespoons finely chopped flat-leaf parsley

2 fennel bulbs, green tops finely chopped, bulbs thinly sliced

sea salt and freshly ground black pepper

250 g (9 oz) linguine

extra virgin olive oil

50 g (2 oz) pine nuts, toasted

To prepare the sardines, first scrape away the scales using a small knife under running water. Remove the back fin, head and tail, and prise out the backbone from head to tail. Slit open the belly, cut out the gut and, using your fingers, carefully cut away any bones that remain. You should have two fillets.

Choose a large frying pan that can accommodate the sardines in one layer, without overlapping.

Heat the olive oil in the pan, and gently cook the garlic until light brown. Add the chilli and parsley, gently place the sardine fillets on top and cook briefly.

Scatter the fennel greens on top of the sardines and season. Do not stir the sauce too much as this will break up the sardines.

Cook the linguine and sliced fennel in a large saucepan of boiling salted water. When the pasta is cooked, drain and add to the sardines. Pour over some extra virgin olive oil and serve immediately, with the pine nuts.

Linguine al Granchio
Linguini with Crab

Serves 10

2 large live male crabs, about 2-3 kg (4.1/2-6.1/2 lb) total weight

3 fresh red chillies, seeded and finely chopped

3 handfuls flat-leaf parsley, finely chopped

juice of 4 lemons

3 garlic cloves, peeled and ground to a paste with a little salt

250 ml (8 fl oz) olive oil

500 g (18 oz) linguine

sea salt and freshly ground black pepper

extra virgin olive oil

Get the fishmonger to kill the crabs for you. In a saucepan large enough to hold both, bring enough water to the boil to cover the crabs. Boil gently for 20 minutes, then remove from the water and leave to cool.

Remove the claws and legs. Break the bodies open carefully. Remove the brown meat from inside the shell and transfer along with any juices to a bowl. Remove the white meat from the claws and legs and add to the brown meat in the bowl. Mix together.

Add the chilli and most of the chopped parsley, the lemon juice and crushed garlic to the crab mixture. Stir in the olive oil. This sauce should be quite liquid.

Cook the linguine in a generous amount of boiling salted water then drain thoroughly. Stir into the crab sauce, but do not reheat. Serve sprinkled with the remaining chopped parsley and a generous amount of extra virgin olive oil.

Linguine Con Cozze al Sugo Rosso
Linguine with Mussels in a Red Sauce

Serves 6

3 kg (6.1/2 lb) mussels, cleaned (see page 15)

4 tablespoons olive oil

4 garlic cloves, peeled and finely sliced

150 ml (5 fl oz) white wine

a handful of flat-leaf parsley, finely chopped

fresh red chilli, seeded and chopped

900 g (2 lb) fresh plum tomatoes, seeded and chopped

a handful of basil, chopped

sea salt and freshly ground black pepper

250 g (9 oz) linguine

extra virgin olive oil

Cook the mussels in half the olive oil over a high heat in a large pan with half the garlic and the wine until they open. Leave the mussels to cool, then remove from their shells. Retain the liquid.

Heat the remaining olive oil and garlic and half the parsley. Fry until the garlic colours, then add the chilli and tomatoes. Cook together gently, reducing the tomatoes to a sauce, about 30 minutes, then add the mussel liquid and return to the boil. Remove from the heat and add the mussels, basil, salt and pepper.

Cook the linguine in a generous amount of boiling salted water, drain thoroughly and add to the mussel sauce.

To serve, pour over a little extra virgin olive oil, and sprinkle with the remaining parsley.

Linguine con Cozze al Sugo Bianco
Linguine with Mussels and White Wine

Serves 6

3 kg (6.1/2 lb) mussels, cleaned (see page 15)

1/3 bottle white wine

4 tablespoons olive oil

2 garlic cloves, peeled and finely chopped

1 dried chilli, crumbled

120 ml (4 fl oz) double cream

sea salt and freshly ground black pepper

250 g (9 oz) linguine

1 bunch flat-leaf parsley, finely chopped

Cook the mussels in the wine and half the olive oil over a high heat in a large saucepan with a lid. Remove from the pan as soon as they open. Leave the mussels to cool then remove three-quarters from their shells. Retain the liquid.

In another pan, heat the remaining olive oil and add the garlic and chilli. Fry gently until the garlic is light brown, then add the mussel liquid and the cream. Cook until reduced by half and thickened. Season with salt and pepper, add the shelled mussels and half the parsley, and remove from the heat.

Meanwhile cook the linguine in a generous amount of boiling salted water, then drain thoroughly. Add to the sauce. Serve topped with the mussels in their shells, and the remaining parsley.

Tagliarini con Trevise

The bitter taste of the cooked trevise and chicory complements the egg tagliarini.

Serves 6

175 g (6 oz) pancetta stesa, cut into matchsticks

2 tablespoons olive oil

50 g (2 oz) butter

2 small red onions, peeled and sliced

2 tablespoons fresh thyme leaves

2 small garlic cloves, peeled and sliced

2 small dried chillies, crumbled

500 g (18 oz) trevise or red radicchio, trimmed and finely sliced

500 g (18 oz) chicory, trimmed and sliced

75 ml (2.1/2 fl oz) white wine

150 ml (5 fl oz) Chicken Stock (see page 54)

120 g (4.1/2 oz) Parmesan, freshly grated

250 g (9 oz) tagliarini

sea salt and freshly ground black pepper

In a large saucepan gently fry the pancetta in half the oil and all the butter until the pancetta releases its fat and begins to colour, about 5 minutes. Add the onion and thyme and continue to fry for a further 5 minutes until the onion is light brown. Add the garlic, chilli and the remaining oil and stir for a minute or two to combine before adding the trevise and chicory. Stir for a few minutes until the colour changes and the trevise wilts. Add the white wine and stock, and bring to the boil. Simmer very gently for 20 minutes to thicken and reduce the liquid then stir in half the Parmesan.

Cook the pasta in a generous amount of boiling salted water, then drain thoroughly. Stir into the sauce, season well, then serve with the remaining Parmesan.

Risotto alla Milanese

This risotto is the accompaniment for Ossobuco in Bianco (see page 216). Risotto alla Milanese calls for the addition of a generous amount of saffron and beef marrow. Just before the Ossobuco is served, add a ladleful of its juices to the risotto.

Serves 6

1 litre (1.3/4 pints) Chicken Stock (see page 54)

sea salt and freshly ground black pepper

150 g (5 oz) butter, at room temperature

2 tablespoons olive oil

1 medium red onion, peeled and very finely chopped

300 g (10 oz) risotto rice

1 teaspoon saffron threads, soaked in a little stock

75 ml (2.1/2 fl oz) extra dry white vermouth

175 g (6 oz) Parmesan, freshly grated

Heat the Chicken Stock and check for seasoning.

Melt 75 g (3 oz) of the butter and all the oil in a large, heavy-bottomed saucepan and gently fry the onion until soft, about 15-20 minutes. Add the rice and, off the heat, stir until the rice becomes totally coated; this takes only a minute. Return to the heat, add 2 or so ladlefuls of hot stock, or just enough to cover the rice, and simmer, stirring, until the rice has absorbed nearly all the liquid. Add the saffron. Continue to add more stock as the previous addition is absorbed. Nearly all of the stock will have been absorbed by the rice; each grain will have a creamy coating, but will remain al dente.

Add the remaining butter in small pieces, the vermouth and the Parmesan, being careful not to overstir. Serve immediately.

Risotto al Salto
Risotto Cake

Serves 6

1 litre (1.3/4 pints) Chicken Stock (see page 54)

sea salt and freshly ground black pepper

120 g (4.1/2 oz) butter, at room temperature

2 tablespoons olive oil

1 beef or veal shin bone, cut open at both ends to reveal the marrow

1 medium red onion, peeled and very finely chopped

300 g (10 oz) risotto rice

Parmesan, freshly grated

Poach the shin bone gently in water for 35-40 minutes. Remove the marrow.

Heat the Chicken Stock and check for seasoning.

Melt 75 g (3 oz) of the butter and all the oil in a large heavy-bottomed pan with the marrow and gently fry the onion until soft, about 15-20 minutes. Thereafter follow method for Risotto alla Milanese.

Spread the cooked risotto out on a flat plate to a thickness of about 2 cm (3/4 in) and leave to cool. Melt the remaining butter in a heavy-bottomed frying pan. Press in the cool rice, in a cake-like layer, about 2.5 cm (1 in) thick. Fry until crisp and browned. Turn out on to a flat plate and cut into wedges. Serve hot, as an accompaniment to Osso Buco (page 216), with freshly grated Parmesan.

Risotto con Carciofi
Risotto with Artichokes

Violetti, the small artichokes with thorny points, are in season from December to early February, and are perfect for this risotto.

Serves 6

8 small globe artichokes, prepared and trimmed (see page 147)

2 garlic cloves, peeled and finely chopped

3 tablespoons olive oil

sea salt and freshly ground black pepper

1 litre (1.3/4 pints) Chicken Stock (see page 54)

150 g (5 oz) butter, at room temperature

1 medium red onion, peeled and very finely chopped

300 g (10 oz) risotto rice

75 ml (2.1/2 fl oz) extra dry white vermouth

175 g (6 oz) Parmesan, freshly grated

Cut the artichokes in half and slice as thinly as possible. Fry gently with the garlic in 1 tablespoon of the olive oil for 5 minutes, stirring continually, then add 120 ml (4 fl oz) water, salt and pepper, and simmer until the water has evaporated.

Heat the Chicken Stock and check for seasoning.

Melt 75 g (3 oz) of the butter in the remaining oil in a large heavy-bottomed saucepan and gently fry the onion until soft, about 15-20 minutes. Add the rice and, off the heat, stir until the rice becomes totally coated, this takes only a minute. Return to the heat, add 2 or so ladlefuls of hot stock or just enough to cover the rice, and simmer, stirring, until the rice has absorbed nearly all the liquid. Continue to add more stock as the previous addition is absorbed. After about 15-20 minutes, nearly all of the stock will have been absorbed by the rice; each grain will have a creamy coating, but will remain al dente.

Add the remaining butter in small pieces, the vermouth, Parmesan and artichokes, being careful not to overstir.

Risotto ai Funghi
Risotto with Mushrooms

Serves 6

100 g (4 oz) dried porcini mushrooms, reconstituted (see page 312)

675 g (1.1/2 lb) medium flat field mushrooms, thickly sliced

7 tablespoons olive oil

3 garlic cloves, peeled and sliced

sea salt and freshly ground black pepper

2 tablespoons chopped fresh basil, marjoram or flat-leaf parsley

juice of 1 lemon

1 litre (1.3/4 pints) Chicken Stock (see page 54)

150 g (5 oz) butter, at room temperature

1 medium red onion, peeled and very finely chopped

300 g (10 oz) risotto rice

75 ml (2.1/2 fl oz) extra dry white vermouth

175 g (6 oz) Parmesan, freshly grated

Heat 4 tablespoons of the olive oil in a large heavy-bottomed frying pan until smoking. Add the sliced fresh mushrooms and fry, stirring constantly, for 15-20 minutes or until the mushrooms have become very dark. Remove and keep warm.

Wipe clean the frying pan. Strain the porcini mushrooms, retaining their juices, rinse and squeeze dry. Heat another tablespoon of olive oil in the pan and gently fry the garlic and porcini. When the garlic begins to colour, carefully pour in half the strained porcini juices and simmer until reduced to 1 tablespoon. Add the rest of the cooked mushrooms, season with salt and pepper and stir to combine the flavours. Add the herbs and lemon juice. Keep warm.

Heat the Chicken Stock and check for seasoning.

Melt 75 g (3 oz) of the butter and the remaining olive oil in another large heavy-bottomed frying pan and gently fry the onion until soft, about 15-20 minutes. Add the rice and, off the heat, stir until the rice becomes totally coated, this takes only a minute. Return to the heat, add the remaining porcini juices and 2 ladlefuls of hot stock or just enough to cover the rice, and simmer, stirring, until the rice has absorbed nearly all the liquid. Continue to add more stock as the previous addition is absorbed. After about 15-20 minutes, nearly all of the stock will have been absorbed by the rice; each grain will have a creamy coating, but will remain al dente.

Add the remaining butter in small pieces, the mushrooms, vermouth and Parmesan, being careful not to overstir. Serve immediately.

Risotto di Zucca
Pumpkin Risotto

Serves 6

850 g (1.1/2 lb) deep yellow pumpkin or squash, whole or 1 large slice, with the skin

sea salt and freshly ground black pepper

1 bunch fresh marjoram or oregano leaves

2 garlic cloves, peeled and thickly sliced

5 tablespoons olive oil

1 litre (1.3/4 pints) Chicken Stock (see page 54)

150 g (5 oz) butter, at room temperature

1 medium red onion, peeled and very finely chopped

300 g (10 oz) risotto rice

75 ml (2.1/2 fl oz) extra dry white vermouth

175 g (6 oz) Parmesan, freshly grated

Preheat the oven to 220°C/425°F/Gas 7.

Remove the seeds and fibre from the centre of the pumpkin, and cut the flesh and skin into large chunks. Place, skin side down, on a baking tray brushed with a little olive oil, season with salt and pepper and scatter over the herbs and the garlic. Pour over 3 tablespoons of oil, cover with foil and bake until soft, about 50 minutes. The pumpkin is ready when it has shrivelled and begun to brown at the edges. Remove from the oven, allow to cool, then scrape the flesh from the skins and reserve with the juices.

Heat the Chicken Stock and check for seasoning.

Melt 75 g (3 oz) of the butter and the remaining olive oil in a large heavy-bottomed frying pan and gently fry the onion until soft, about 15-20 minutes. Add the rice and, off the heat, stir until the rice becomes totally coated, this takes only a minute. Return to the heat, add 2 or so ladlefuls of hot stock or just enough to cover the rice, and simmer, stirring, until the rice has absorbed nearly all the liquid. Continue to add more stock as the previous addition is absorbed. After about 15-20 minutes, nearly all the stock will have been absorbed by the rice; each grain will have a creamy coating, but will remain al dente.

Add the remaining butter in small pieces, the pumpkin, vermouth and Parmesan, being careful not to overstir. Serve immediately.

Risotto con Fiori di Zucchini
Risotto with Zucchini Flowers

This summer risotto with young zucchini and the male zuchini flowers is both delicate and beautiful.

Serves 6

12 male zucchini flowers

6 small young zucchini

1 litre (1.3/4 pints) Chicken Stock (see page 54)

sea salt and freshly ground black pepper

150 g (5 oz) butter, at room temperature

2 tablespoons olive oil

1 medium red onion, peeled and very finely chopped

300 g (10 oz) risotto rice

75 ml (2.1/2 fl oz) extra dry white vermouth

175 g (6 oz) Parmesan, freshly grated

1 handful fresh basil leaves

Prepare the flowers by removing the stamens and spiky sepals. Tear each flower vertically into 4 strands. Brush to get rid of any dust or insects, but do not wash. Slice the zucchini into very fine discs, as thin as the flower strands.

Heat the Chicken Stock and check for seasoning.

Melt 75 g (3 oz) of the butter and all the oil in a large heavy-bottom pan and gently fry the onion until soft, about 15-20 minutes. Add the rice and, off the heat, stir until the rice becomes totally coated, this only takes a minute. Return to the heat, add 2 or so ladlefuls of hot stock or just enough to cover the rice and simmer, stirring, until the rice has absorbed nearly all the liquid. Continue to add more stock as the previous addition is absorbed. After about 20 minutes, add first the zucchini slices and then the flower strands, along with the last two or three ladlefuls of stock. The zucchini should have a little bite; the flowers will disappear and the rice will have a creamy coating but will remain al dente.

Add the remaining butter, in small pieces, the vermouth, Parmesan and basil leaves, being careful not to overstir.

Risotto al Amarone di Valpolicella

Serves 6

300 ml (10 fl oz) Chicken Stock (see page 54)

sea salt and coarsely ground black pepper

150 g (5 oz) butter, at room temperature

2 medium red onions, peeled and chopped

300 g (10 oz) risotto rice

600 ml (21 fl oz) bottle Amarone di Valpolicella wine

150 g (5 oz) Parmesan, freshly grated

a little double cream

Heat the Chicken Stock, and check for seasoning.

Melt two-thirds of the butter in a large heavy-bottomed pan, and gently fry the onion for about 20 minutes and light brown. Add the rice and stir to coat, this takes only a minute.

Increase the heat, pour in 175 ml (6 fl oz) of the wine, and let it reduce to a syrup. Add the hot stock, ladle by ladle, stirring all the time, only adding more when the rice has absorbed the previous addition.

When the rice is almost cooked, and all the stock has been absorbed, gradually add the remaining wine. The rice should immediately take up the colour of the wine.

Add half the Parmesan, the remaining butter or a little cream, and season, taking care not to overstir. Serve with the rest of the Parmesan.

Risotto Primavera

As these vegetables are so young, we add half of them at the very end to emphasise the fresh taste of spring

Serves 6

225 g (8 oz) each of asparagus, peas, green beans and zucchini

sea salt and freshly ground black pepper

1 litre (1.3/4 pints) Chicken Stock (see page 54)

1 medium red onion, peeled and finely chopped

2 tablespoons olive oil

300 g (10 oz) risotto rice

75 ml (2.1/2 fl oz) extra dry white vermouth

100 g (4 oz) butter

175 g (6 oz) Parmesan, freshly grated

Cut off the tips of the asparagus, and chop the spears and the beans into 2.5 cm (1 in) pieces. Pod the peas.

Cut the zucchini, lengthways into four, and slice to the same size as the green beans.

Take half the vegetables, and blanch in plenty of boiling salted water.

Heat the Chicken Stock, and check for seasoning.

In a large heavy-bottomed saucepan cook the onion in the olive oil until soft but not brown, about 10 minutes. Add the rice and stir for 2 minutes to coat completely with oil. Add enough hot stock to cover the rice and cook gently, adding more stock as it is absorbed. Season with salt and pepper. After about 10 minutes, add the uncooked vegetables, stir, and add more stock. Cook for a further 5 minutes.

Pour in the vermouth and stir, then add the blanched vegetables, the butter and the cheese, taking care not to overstir. The risotto should be moist and creamy. Check the seasoning and serve with more grated Parmesan.

Risotto Nero

Serves 6

1 litre (1.3/4 pints) Fish Stock (see page 55)

sea salt and freshly ground black pepper

75 g (3 oz) butter

4 garlic cloves, peeled and finely chopped

300 g (10 oz) risotto rice

120 ml (4 fl oz) white wine

3 sachets squid or cuttlefish ink

2 tablespoons finely chopped flat-leaf parsley

Heat the Fish Stock, and check for seasoning.

Melt the butter in a saucepan and fry the garlic for 1 minute. Add the rice and continue to cook gently, stirring, for a further minute. Pour in the white wine and cook until it has been absorbed by the rice. Add a ladle of hot fish stock, stirring continually until it too has been absorbed. Continue to add more fish stock until the rice is al dente, then add the squid ink. When there is only one ladle of stock left, turn off the heat and add this remaining stock. Stir in the parsley and season with salt and pepper.

Variations

Add about 450 g (1 lb) small squid, hand size. Clean (see page 208) and cut the body sacs into thin tagliatelle type strips, and separate the tentacles. Heat 1 tablespoon olive oil until very hot, throw in the squid pieces and stir-fry for no more than 30 seconds. Remove and season.

Make the risotto as above, using an extra clove of garlic. Add the squid to the risotto as you stir in the squid ink.

Pol

enta

3

Just as bread is important in Tuscany, pasta in Emilia Romana and rice in the Veneto, polenta is the essential staple of the northernmost region of Italy. Like bread, pasta and rice, polenta can be transformed by the method of cooking.

At the River Cafe we only make polenta when in season and either grill it or serve it wet with butter and parmesan. We cook it wet to go with the recipes that have a lot of juice which will be soaked up by the polenta, such as game birds, sausages with tomato sauce, field and wild mushrooms. Polenta which has been grilled has a crust with a soft texture inside which is delicious with any of our sauces, salads, or braised vegetables.

As you must search for the best rice or pasta flour you must also find the best polenta flour. Bramanta polenta is an organic mixture of three types of maize kernels. When cooking the texture is grainy, the colour deep orange/yellow and there is a wonderful perfume of simmering corn.

On our first wine-tasting trip to Italy, in a restaurant in Piedmont, we ate a dish of polenta that was unlike any we had ever had before. We had to find out where it came from and finally tracked down the mill where it was ground. This polenta as well as their pasta flour is now imported into this country by our wine merchant, Winecellars.

Polenta

Serves 6-8

350 g (12 oz) polenta flour

1.75-2 litres (3-3.1/2 pints) water

sea salt and freshly ground black pepper

150 g (5 oz) butter, at room temperature

200 g (7 oz) Parmesan, freshly grated

Put the polenta flour in a jug with a ladle so that it can be poured in a steady stream.

Bring the water to a boil in a large saucepan and add 1 teaspoon of salt. Lower the heat to a simmer and slowly add the polenta flour, stirring with a whisk until completely blended. It will now start to bubble volcanically. Reduce the heat to as low as possible, and cook the polenta, stirring from time to time with a wooden spoon to prevent a skin forming on the top, for about 40-45 minutes. The polenta is cooked when it falls away from the sides of the pan and has become very dense and thick.

Stir in the butter and Parmesan and season generously with salt and pepper.

Polenta alla Griglia
Grilled Polenta

Serves 6-8

Make the polenta as described opposite, omitting the butter and Parmesan. When ready, transfer to a large flat baking tray or plate, and spread out to form a cake about 2 cm (3/4 in) thick. Leave until completely cold, then cut into wedges or slices.

Preheat a grill to very hot. Brush the pieces of polenta on both sides with olive oil and grill for 3 minutes on each side or until crisp and brown.

Serve in any of the ways described in the following illustrated pages.

Grilled Polenta with prosciutto di San Daniele

Grilled Polenta with asparagus and parmesan

Grilled Polenta with marinated black olives and dried chillies

Wet Polenta with gorgonzola, mascarpone and fresh marjoram

Grilled Polenta with mushrooms and thyme

Grilled Polenta with fresh chilli and rocket

Wet Polenta with partridge, red wine and Parmesan

Grilled Polenta with anchovy, rosemary, lemon and olive oil

Veget
and S

ables

alads

4

In many Italian meals, risottos, pastas, and soups are followed by vegetables or salads rather than meat or fish. Traditionally, it would have been unthinkable to start a meal with anything other than a soup or pasta but nowadays a heavier main course may be preceded by a salad or one of the vegetable dishes in this chapter.

When entering a restaurant in Italy you will often see a large table full of seasonal vegetables. Some have been grilled and then marinated with fresh herbs, some cooked slowly in oil, or combined with others as in the heavenly vignole of artichokes, peas and broadbeans, or simply boiled ready to be dressed with oil and lemon. There are bowls of various leaves, rocket, dandelion, or chicoria, depending on the season and region.

We think very carefully about the vegetables we put with our meat or fish. The choice will depend on the season, the method on the taste and texture of what it is going with. In the winter, if we are grilling bass, a vegetable such as fennel will be slow cooked in olive oil, while in summer we might serve it with zucchini trifolati.

Ricotta al Forno

This is a bright green ricotta soufflé with a black olive crust. It can be made without a food processor.

Serves 6

500 g (18 oz) fresh ricotta cheese

2 handfuls fresh basil

1 handful fresh mint

1 handful flat-leaf parsley

120 ml (4 fl oz) double cream

2 eggs

sea salt and freshly ground black pepper

150 g (5 oz) Parmesan, freshly grated

12 black olives, stoned and chopped

Preheat the oven to 190°C/375°F/Gas 5.

Using a little butter and some extra grated Parmesan, coat a 30 cm (10 in) spring-release tin. Shake off the excess cheese.

Put the herbs into the bowl of a food processor and put half of the ricotta and cream on the top. Blend until bright green. Add the remainder of the ricotta and cream and, while blending, add the eggs one by one. Season with salt and pepper. Finally fold in the Parmesan.

Spoon the mixture into the tin and spread the olives over the top. Bake in the preheated oven for 20 minutes. The torte should rise and have a brown crust but be soft in the centre. Serve immediately.

Torta di Ricotta e Bietola con Pasta Frolla

We make this pizza with pasta frolla, a type of flaky pastry, rather than bread dough.

Serves 8

about 1 kg (2.1/4 lb) Swiss chard

sea salt and freshly ground black pepper

extra virgin olive oil

3 red onions, peeled and sliced

1 generous bunch fresh thyme

2 garlic cloves, peeled and chopped

250 g (9 oz) ricotta cheese

1 egg yolk

2 tablespoons crème fraîche

150 g (5 oz) Parmesan, freshly grated

100 g (4 oz) stoned black olives

For the pasta frolla (flaky pastry)

360 g (12.1/2 oz) plain flour

225 g (8 oz) very cold butter, cut into small pieces

sea salt

6 tablespoons ice-cold water

Make the pasta frolla. Put the flour and butter pieces in a food processor with a little salt, and pulse until it has the consistency of breadcrumbs. Immediately add the water and pulse for a second to combine. Gather the dough together into a ball, wrap in cling film and place in the refrigerator for 1 hour.

Heat the oven to 200°C/400°F/Gas 6, and have ready a large flat baking tray.

Separate the leaves and stalks of the chard. Roughly slice the stalks and blanch in boiling salted water for 2 minutes, then blanch the leaves for about 1 minute. Drain well.

Fry the onion gently in about 3 tablespoons of olive oil, until light brown. Add half the thyme and the chard stalks and cook together for a few minutes to combine the flavours. Keep warm.

Heat a further 2 tablespoons of oil in a separate pan and fry the garlic until light brown. Add the blanched chard leaves and cook briefly to combine the flavours. Season.

Break up the ricotta with a fork and season with salt and pepper. Mix the egg yolk, crème fraîche and 100 g (4 oz) of the Parmesan together.

Coarsely grate the pastry and quickly press on to the flat baking tray to a thickness of 5 mm (1/4 in) – the edges can be quite rough. Bake blind in the preheated oven for 10 minutes.

Sprinkle the onion mixture, then the ricotta mixture over the pastry. Spread the chard leaves on top, followed by the olives and remaining sprigs of thyme. Dribble over the crème fraîche mixture and a generous amount of olive oil. Add the remaining Parmesan, and return to the oven for a further 10-15 minutes. Serve immediately cut into pizza-like squares.

Gnocchi Verdi con Ricotta
Ricotta and Spinach Gnocchi

We have adapted the traditional recipe by adding marjoram to the spinach, and reducing the amount of flour which results in lighter gnocchi.

Serves 6

50 g (2 oz) butter

a bunch of fresh marjoram

500 g (18 oz) blanched spinach leaves, squeezed dry

sea salt

200 g (7 oz) fresh ricotta cheese

90 g (3.1/2 oz) plain flour

3 egg yolks

1/2 nutmeg, grated

150 g (5 oz) Parmesan, freshly grated

Sage Butter (see page 68)

Melt the butter, add the marjoram, and cook for a minute. Add the spinach, and stir to combine the flavours. Season, leave to cool, then chop roughly.

In a large bowl, lightly beat the ricotta with a fork, then sieve in the flour. Add the egg yolks, the nutmeg and Parmesan and finally fold in the cooled spinach mixture until well combined. Taste for seasoning.

Dust a baking tray with flour.

Using two dessertspoons, take a small spoonful of mixture and, using the one spoon, mould the mixture so that it forms a gnoccho. Place on the floured baking tray. The gnocchi should all be the same size, about 2 cm (3/4 in) in diameter.

Bring a large pan of water to the boil, then lower the heat to a simmer.

Gently place the gnocchi in the water in batches – it is important not to overcrowd the pan. When the gnocchi come back to the surface, remove carefully with a slotted spoon and briefly place the spoon on kitchen paper to drain off excess water.

Serve immediately on warm plates with Sage Butter and extra Parmesan.

Asparagi e Torta di Gorgonzola

Serves 6

1 kg (2.1/4 lb) asparagus, trimmed weight

sea salt and freshly ground black pepper

100 g (4 oz) Parmesan, freshly grated

For the sauce

25 g (1 oz) butter

200 g (7 oz) Torta di Gorgonzola

50 g (2 oz) mascarpone

a small handful of fresh oregano or basil leaves, chopped

Melt the butter very gently in a medium-sized pan, then add the Torta di Gorgonzola. Heat until softened but do not allow it to become liquid – it should be just warm, no more. Add the mascarpone, the herbs, a little salt and pepper, and remove from the heat. This should only take a matter of seconds.

Briefly blanch the asparagus in a generous amount of boiling salted water. Drain, dry and place on warm plates. Pour over the sauce, and serve with Parmesan.

Variation

This sauce can also be used with Grilled Polenta (see page 121).

Asparagi con Uova

We would only make this dish if we had fantastic eggs. To us that means eggs freshly laid from a real farm. This is a rare luxury.

Serves 6

1 kg (2.1/4 lb) thin asparagus, trimmed weight

sea salt and freshly ground black pepper

6 egg yolks, at room temperature

100 g (4 oz) unsalted butter, melted

120 g (4.1/2 oz) Parmesan in the piece, very thinly shaved

Bring a large pot of water to the boil with a generous amount of salt. Blanch the asparagus for about 3 minutes, depending on the thickness. Drain and place on warm plates. Gently place the egg yolks on the tips of the asparagus, without breaking the yolks and season with black pepper. Pour on the warm butter, and cover with shavings of Parmesan.

Vignole

Vignole is found on the menus of restaurants in Rome in spring and is one of the River Cafe's favourite starters.

Serves 8

1.5 kg (3.1/4 lb) each of peas and broad beans in their pods

8 small baby globe artichokes with their stalks

2 large handfuls fresh mint

4 tablespoons olive oil

50 g (2 oz) butter

2 medium red onions, peeled and finely chopped

1 thick slice prosciutto

sea salt and freshly ground black pepper

8 thin slices prosciutto, cut into ribbons

extra virgin olive oil

Bruschetta

8 slices pugliese bread

1 garlic clove, peeled and halved

Shell the peas and broad beans and keep to one side. Blanch the artichokes whole in boiling water for 5 minutes, or until you can pull of an outer leaf with a sharp tug. They should not be completely cooked at this stage. Remove and cool. Remove the mint leaves from their stalks and chop half of them.

In a separate pan, blanch the broad beans for 2 minutes.

In a large heavy-bottomed saucepan, heat 2 tablespoons of the olive oil with the butter, then gently fry the chopped onion until light brown. Add the peas and stir gently for a minute to coat with the oil and the onion. Pour in enough water to just cover, and place the thick slice of prosciutto on the top. Gently simmer for 20-40 minutes, or until the peas are soft, adding more water if the level falls below that of the peas and prosciutto.

When the artichokes have cooled, peel off the outer tough leaves, and cut off the stalk about 5 cm (2 in) from the base. If the stalk seems stringy, scrape away the outer layer; the core of the stalk is always tender. Cut off the top tough part of the cone, then slice the artichoke lengthways into eighths.

In a separate pan heat the remaining olive oil, add the sliced artichokes and fry, stirring, until they become light brown. Add the whole mint leaves, salt and pepper to taste, and a ladle of stock or water. Continue to cook for a minute or two.

Remove and discard the prosciutto from the peas; it will have imparted its flavour during the simmering. Add the artichoke pieces and juices to the peas, along with the broad beans and the chopped mint. Heat through but do not cook as this will toughen the beans. Remove from the heat and stir in the ribbons of prosciutto and about 85 ml (3 fl oz) extra virgin olive oil.

To make the bruschetta, toast the bread on both sides and rub gently on one side only with the garlic. Pour on more extra virgin olive oil and serve with the Vignole.

Peperoni con Acciughe e Capperi
Char-grilled Peppers with Anchovy and Capers

Serves 6

6 red and 6 yellow peppers

50 g (4 oz) salted capers, prepared (see page 306)

100 g (4 oz) salted anchovies, prepared (see page 304)

3 garlic cloves, peeled and cut into slivers

a handful of fresh basil or marjoram

freshly ground black pepper

extra virgin olive oil

3 slices pugliese bread, cut in half, toasted and rubbed with garlic

Grill the whole peppers on all sides. When the skins are entirely black, place the peppers in a plastic bag and seal.

When cool, remove the blackened skin by rubbing the peppers in your hands. Do not worry if they fall apart. Then remove the seeds and cores.

Layer the peppers with slivers of garlic, capers, anchovies, basil, black pepper and a generous amount of extra virgin olive oil. The final layer should have all the ingredients visible.

Serve with the bruschetta.

Verdura Mista in Graticola
Marinated Grilled Vegetables

Serves 6

450 g (1 lb) aubergine

450 g (1 lb) zucchini

450 g (1 lb) each of red and yellow peppers, skinned (see page 140)

sea salt and freshly ground black pepper

extra virgin olive oil (up to 200 ml /7 fl oz)

juice of 2 lemons

2 garlic cloves, peeled and crushed in a little sea salt

a handful of fresh basil or marjoram

Cut the aubergine lengthways into eighths and place in a colander with some sea salt. Cut the zucchini lengthways into sixths or eighths depending on size, add some salt, and place in a separate colander. Leave both to drain of any bitter juices, for a minimum of 30 minutes. Rinse and dry well.

Break the skinned peppers into sixths, and place on a dish.

Place the aubergine and zucchini pieces on the hottest part of the grill and grill on both sides, seasoning at the same time with salt and pepper. The aubergine in particular requires care – it needs to be cooked, but should not be allowed to burn. To test, gently press with a finger; if it resists, it is not done. When it is cooked, keep separate with the zucchini.

Mix the olive oil with the lemon juice and garlic, and pour over the individual vegetables, gently lifting to coat them. Combine all the seasoned vegetables in a large bowl with the basil leaves, turn over once, and taste for seasoning – it should be robust.

Fritto Misto
Deep-fried Vegetables

Elizabeth David's recipe for batter is the best we know. It differs from traditional Italian batters in that it only uses egg whites and is therefore exceptionally light.

Serves 6

12 male zucchini flowers

2 aubergines, sliced into 1 cm (1/2 in) rounds

3 zucchini, trimmed and cut into quarters lengthways

24 large sage leaves

12 salted anchovies, prepared (see page 304)

sunflower oil for deep-frying

3 lemons

For the batter

225 g (8 oz) plain flour

4 tablespoons extra virgin olive oil

about 300 ml (10 fl oz) warm water

sea salt and freshly ground black pepper

4 large egg whites

To make the batter, sieve the flour into a large bowl. Pour the olive oil into a well in the centre and slowly stir with a wooden spoon to combine the flour into the oil. Add a little warm water until the batter is the consistency of double cream. Season and let stand for at least 2 hours in a cool place.

Prepare the zucchini flowers by removing the stamens and spiky sepals.

Place the aubergine and zucchini in separate colanders with some salt and allow to drain of any bitter juices for a minimum of 30 minutes. Rinse and dry well.

Wash the sage leaves and dry well. Rinse the anchovy fillets. Make a 'sandwich' of two sage leaves with a piece of anchovy fillet in between. Press together: the wetness of the anchovies will hold the sage leaves.

Heat the sunflower oil to 180°C/350°F.

Just before cooking, beat the egg white until stiff and fold into the batter. Dip the aubergine, zucchini and flowers into the batter, allowing any excess batter to drain back into the bowl (the vegetables should only be thinly coated), and fry until light brown, then drain on kitchen paper.

Fry the anchovy 'sandwiches' directly in the oil without any batter.

Serve with half a lemon for each person.

Carciofi alla Giudea
Deep-fried Whole Artichokes

This traditional Jewish dish from Rome is stunning in its simplicity and boldness.

Serves 6

12 small globe artichokes with their stalks

sea salt and freshly ground black pepper

sunflower oil for deep-frying

3 lemons

Using a small, sharp knife remove the tougher outer leaves of the artichokes and, if necessary trim, the spikes from the top. Cut the stalks, leaving about 5 cm (2 in) and peel.

Using your fingers, gently prise open each artichoke, turn it upside down and, while pressing down with one hand, pull out the leaves with the other. The aim is to open up and flatten the artichoke. Season the opened surface with salt and pepper.

Heat the oil to 180°C/350°F. Plunge two or three artichokes into the hot oil at a time, and fry just until the leaves curl up and become crisp, about 3-4 minutes. Drain well on kitchen paper.

Serve with lemon halves.

Carciofi Marinati
Marinated Globe Artichokes

Serves 6

12 small globe artichokes with their stalks

sea salt and freshly ground black pepper

1 small bunch each of marjoram, thyme, oregano and summer savory

2 heads garlic, cloves peeled and thickly sliced

extra virgin olive oil

lemon juice

With a small, sharp knife, prepare the artichokes by first cutting the stalks, leaving about 5 cm (2 in), then peel them, leaving only the pale tender centre. Cut or break off the tough outer leaves, starting at the base, so that you are left with the pale inner heart. Trim the tops if tough or sharp.

Cut the artichokes in half from tip to stalk. Feel with your finger and if the choke is at all prickly, remove with a teaspoon.

Blanch in boiling salted water for about 5 minutes, or until a leaf pulls out easily. Drain and dry well. Layer in a large bowl with the herbs, garlic, salt and pepper. Cover completely with extra virgin olive oil – you will probably need about 1 litre (1.3/4 pints) – and lemon juice and marinate for a minimum of 3 hours. They will keep for up to 4-5 days.

Serve with a little of the oil and lots of lemon juice.

Carciofi Trifolati

The translation of 'Trifolato' is to slice like truffles and cook with oil, parsley and garlic.

Serves 4

4 globe artichokes

1/2 lemon (optional)

3 tablespoons olive oil

2 garlic cloves, peeled and chopped

sea salt and freshly ground black pepper

1 tablespoon chopped mint

1 tablespoon chopped flat-leaf parsley

2 dried chillies, crumbled

To prepare the artichokes, first snap off the stalks, then peel or break away from the base the tough outer leaves until you are left with the pale inner heart. Scrape away the prickly choke and cut the artichokes into sixths. The slices will discolour, which does not alter the taste. Rub with the cut lemon if you prefer.

Heat the oil in a large heavy saucepan or frying pan with a lid, over a high heat until it smokes. Add the artichoke pieces and stir constantly until they are light brown, about 5 minutes. Lower the heat to medium, add the garlic and when it starts to colour, add about 3 tablespoons water, and salt and pepper. Cover with the lid and cook until the water has evaporated, about 5 minutes.

Add the mint, parsley, chilli and lemon juice and stir.

Broccoli con Acciughe
Broccoli with Anchovy

Best with English purple sprouting broccoli.

Serves 6

900 g (2 lb) broccoli, trimmed and cut lengthways, keeping as many leaves as possible

sea salt and freshly ground black pepper

4 tablespoons olive oil

3 garlic cloves, peeled and thinly sliced

2 small dried chillies, crumbled

12 whole salted anchovies, prepared (see page 304)

juice of 1 lemon

Bruschetta

6 slices pugliese bread, cut at an angle

1 garlic clove, peeled and halved

extra virgin olive oil

3 lemons

Briefly blanch the broccoli in a generous amount of boiling salted water. Drain well.

Heat the oil in a large pan and gently fry the garlic until it begins to colour. Add the chilli, turn off the heat, add the anchovies and stir until the anchovies have dissolved.

Add the blanched broccoli and season with black pepper. Return to the heat and add a small amount of boiling water to release the anchovy and make a sauce. Stir and cook for 5-10 minutes; the broccoli should be soft. Add the lemon juice.

Make the bruschetta by toasting the bread on both sides and then rubbing with the garlic. Pile the broccoli mixture on to the bruschetta and pour over some extra virgin olive oil. Serve with lemon quarters.

Carciofi alla Romana
Artichokes Roman Style

Serves 6

12 small or 6 large globe artichokes

lemon juice

250 ml (8 fl oz) olive oil

For the stuffing

3 tablespoons finely chopped flat-leaf parsley

3 tablespoons finely chopped fresh mint

3 garlic cloves, peeled and crushed with sea salt

6 tablespoons olive oil

coarsely ground black pepper

1 1/2 lemons, quartered

Prepare the artichokes as described on pages 146 and 147.

For the stuffing, mix all the ingredients together, and season well. Press this mixture inside the centre of each artichoke .

Pour the olive oil into a heavy stainless-steel saucepan large enough to contain all the artichokes. Place in the artichokes, stuffed side down, jammed together so they stay upright. Scatter any excess stuffing over the top. Add enough water to come one-third of the way up the globes, and bring to the boil. Reduce the heat, cover with a sheet of greaseproof paper, place the lid on top, and cook gently for about 30 minutes until the water has evaporated and the artichokes have begun to brown at the bottom. The timing will depend on the size and freshness of the artichokes. Test for tenderness using a sharp pointed knife. You may need to add more water and cook for longer. Ideally, the result should be tender artichokes that have begun to caramelise in the oil. Serve with lemon quarters.

Insalata di Carciofi Crudi
Raw Artichoke Salad

Serves 6

6 small globe artichokes, prepared (see page 147)

juice of 3 lemons

3 tablespoons extra virgin olive oil, plus extra to serve

sea salt and freshly ground black pepper

100 g (4 oz) Parmesan in the piece, very thinly shaved

Finely slice the artichokes and place in a bowl of water with the juice of 2 lemons.

Make the dressing with the remaining lemon juice and the olive oil, seasoned with salt and pepper.

When ready to serve, drain and dry the artichokes and pour over the dressing.

Cover with thin shavings of Parmesan, and pour over more extra virgin olive oil.

Insalata di Topinambur
Jerusalem Artichoke Salad

Serves 6

225 g (8 oz) Jerusalem artichokes

3 lemons

1 handful fresh dandelion leaves

2 heads red chicory or 1 small radicchio

1 handful baby spinach leaves or rocket

8 tablespoons extra virgin olive oil

8 drops white truffle oil

sea salt and freshly ground black pepper

200 g (7 oz) Parmesan in the piece, very thinly shaved

Peel the artichokes and put in a bowl of water with the juice of 1 lemon.

Wash the salad leaves, dry thoroughly, and then place in a bowl.

Cut the artichokes into fine slivers, the finer the better. Put them in a separate bowl. Mix together the juice of the remaining lemons, the olive oil and truffle oil. Season and pour half over the artichokes.

Pour the remaining dressing over the salad leaves. Divide the dressed leaves between individual plates, and cover with the artichoke and then the Parmesan slivers. Dribble over a few drops of truffle oil.

Zucchini alla Scapece

Carefully made wine vinegar is really important in this recipe

Serves 6

1.5 kg (3 lb) zucchini, trimmed

sea salt and freshly ground black pepper

sunflower oil for deep-frying

2 tablespoons red wine vinegar

2 large garlic cloves, peeled and finely cut into fine slivers

1 fresh red chilli, seeded and cut into fine slivers

2 tablespoons roughly chopped fresh mint

4 tablespoons extra virgin olive oil

Thinly slice the zucchini into discs: the thinner they are, the crisper they will be when fried. Place in a large bowl of iced water for at least 30 minutes. Drain in a colander and dry well.

Heat the oil 180°C/350°F. Fry the zucchini in batches until light brown and crisp, then remove immediately and place on kitchen paper to drain. Avoid putting too many in the oil at one time, as this will cause the temperature of the oil to drop.

Place the zucchini on a large flat plate and shake over the vinegar, then scatter over the garlic and chilli and finally the mint.

Zucchini Trifolati

The interesting thing about this recipe is the addition of water to the oil which makes the zucchini have a creamy consistency.

Serves 6

18 small zucchini, trimmed and cut at an angle into 3-4 slices

3 tablespoons olive oil

2 garlic cloves, peeled and sliced

a handful of mint or basil leaves, roughly chopped

sea salt and freshly ground black pepper

Heat the oil in a large frying pan, add the zucchini and cook slowly for 15-20 minutes. When brown on all sides, add 125 ml (4 fl oz) boiling water and stir, scraping and combining the brown juices that have formed on the bottom of the pan until all the water has been absorbed and the zucchini are soft. Add the mint or basil, season with salt and pepper and serve.

Pomodoro al Forno con Basilico

Serves 6

12 ripe fresh plum tomatoes

4 garlic cloves, peeled

sea salt and freshly ground black pepper

6 tablespoons chopped fresh basil

olive oil

Preheat the oven to 120°C/250°F/Gas 1/2.

Slice the tomatoes in half lengthways, and scoop out the seeds. Crush the garlic with a little salt to a smooth paste. Add the basil and some black pepper.

Spread this mixture evenly on the cut surfaces of the tomatoes. Place upright in a suitable ovenproof dish, and pour in enough olive oil to come one-third of the way up the tomatoes. Cook in the preheated oven for 3 hours or longer. The result should be almost like sun-dried tomatoes as they will shrivel as they cook. Check the olive oil level occasionally. The longer the tomatoes cook, the better.

Insalata di Pane, Pomodoro e Basilico
Toasted Tuscan Bread Salad with Tomatoes and Basil

Serves 6

1 ciabatta loaf

1 kg (2.1/4 lb) ripe fresh plum tomatoes (they must have a strong flavour)

250 ml (8 fl oz) extra virgin olive oil

2 tablespoons best quality red wine vinegar

2 garlic cloves, peeled and crushed with a little sea salt

sea salt and freshly ground black pepper

a handful fresh basil leaves

juice of 1/2 lemon

Preheat the oven to 240°C/475°F/Gas 9, or the highest it will go.

Roughly tear the loaf into eighths and place on a baking tray. Bake in the oven until dry and toasted on the outside, but soft in the centre (no more than 5 minutes). Place in a bowl.

Take four of the tomatoes and, using your hands, squeeze them over the toasted bread. Mix together a dressing using half the olive oil, the vinegar, crushed garlic and some salt and pepper. Pour the dressing over the toasted bread and tomato and toss.

Skin and seed the remaining tomatoes, retaining their juices, slice lengthways into eighths and add them, with the basil, to the bread mixture. Finally, add the lemon juice to bring out the flavour of the tomatoes and pour over the remaining olive oil.

Insalata di Finocchio
Raw Fennel Salad

Serves 6

6 fennel bulbs, outer leaves removed

3 tablespoons balsamic vinegar

75 g (3 oz) Parmesan in the piece, broken into very small pieces

Trim the herb tops of the fennel bulbs, then slice as finely as possible lengthways so that each slice remains attached to the stalk. Put in a bowl and toss with the balsamic vinegar and the Parmesan.

Finocchio alla Griglia
Grilled Fennel Salad

Serves 6

6 large fennel bulbs, outer leaves removed

1/2 lemon

Oil and Lemon Dressing (see page 166)

Keep the green herb tops of the fennel bulbs. Slice the fennel bulbs as finely as possible lengthways so that each slice remains attached to the stalk. Place in a bowl of iced water with the lemon half to prevent discoloration.

Preheat a grill. Dry the fennel slices in a cloth and grill on both sides until they have char marks but remain al dente.

Place in a bowl and toss with the olive oil and lemon dressing, and the chopped green fennel herb. Serve at room temperature.

Panzanella

Panzanella is a traditional Tuscan summer salad. At its most simple it is just strong white bread, green peppery olive oil and delicious ripe summer tomatoes. The addition of peppers, anchovies, olives and capers make it more delicious and interesting.

Serves 6

3 stale ciabatta loaves

1 kg (2.1/4 lb) fresh plum tomatoes

4 garlic cloves, peeled and crushed to a paste with a little sea salt

sea salt and freshly ground black pepper

Tuscan extra virgin olive oil

4 tablespoons red wine vinegar

3 red peppers

3 yellow peppers

2 fresh red chillies (optional)

100 g (4 oz) salted capers, prepared (see page 306)

100 g (4 oz) salted anchovies, prepared (see page 304)

150 g (5 oz) black olives, stoned

1 large bunch basil

Cut the bread into rough, thick slices, and place in a large bowl.

Skin, halve and seed the tomatoes, into a sieve over a bowl to retain the tomato juice. Season the juice with the garlic and some black pepper, then add 250 ml (8 fl oz) of the olive oil and 2-3 tablespoons of the red wine vinegar. Pour the seasoned tomato juices over the bread and toss until the bread has absorbed all the liquid. Depending on the staleness of the bread, more liquid may be required, in which case add more olive oil.

Grill the peppers whole until blackened all over (see page 140), then skin, seed and cut into eighths lengthways. If using, grill the chillies until blackened, then skin, seed and chop finely.

Rinse the salt from the capers and soak in the remaining red wine vinegar. Separate the anchovies into fillets.

In a large dish, make a layer of some of the soaked bread, and top with some of all the other ingredients, then cover with another layer of bread and continue until all the bread and other ingredients have been used up. The final layer should have the peppers, tomatoes, capers, anchovies and olives all visible. Leave for an hour at room temperature before serving with more extra virgin olive oil.

Radicchio alla Griglia
Grilled Radicchio

Serves 6

3 medium heads of radicchio

sea salt and freshly ground black pepper

Olive Oil and Vinegar Dressing (see page 166)

1 small bunch fresh marjoram, parsley or basil

Preheat the grill.

Carefully peel open and separate the whole leaves of radicchio. Place the leaves in a single layer on the grill. Season and turn over immediately just to wilt, not to blacken. Place in an ovenproof dish and pour over the dressing. Turn to coat the leaves, add the herbs, and bake in an oven heated to 180°C/350°F/Gas 4 for 15 minutes.

Insalata Invernale
Winter Salad

In December and January, before the flowers form on the dandelion, pick the small centre leaves from wild plants.

Serves 6

a handful each of dandelion, rocket, trevise or radicchio, red or white chicory or young
  spinach, lamb's lettuce

Oil and Lemon Dressing (see page 166)

Wash and pick over the rocket and dandelion leaves. Separate the trevise or radicchio and chicory leaves from their stalks and check for dirt. Mix all the leaves together in a bowl and toss with the dressing.

Insalata Estiva
Summer Salad

The ingredients for this salad depend on the wild leaves and sprouting vegetables you can obtain.

Serves 6

a handful each of wild rocket, sorrel, young beet leaves, escarole, cavolo nero, spinach, or

young Swiss chard

Oil and Lemon Dressing (see page 166)

Pick over and wash the leaves. Dry, then mix together and toss with the dressing.

Oil and Lemon Dressing

These quantities are just a guide. If the oil is very young or the lemon juice mild, you will have to adjust by tasting.

6 tablespoons extra virgin olive oil

2 tablespoons lemon juice

sea salt and freshly ground black pepper

Oil, Lemon, Vinegar and Garlic Dressing

6 tablespoons extra virgin olive oil

1 tablespoon lemon juice

1 tablespoon white/red wine vinegar

1 garlic clove, peeled and crushed with a little sea salt

freshly ground black pepper

Olive Oil and Vinegar Dressing

6 tablespoons extra virgin olive oil

2-3 tablespoons red wine or balsamic vinegar

freshly ground black pepper

Patate al Forno con Pancetta
Potato and Pancetta Gratin

Serves 6

100 g (4 oz) pancetta affumicata, thinly sliced

4 tablespoons olive oil

4 garlic cloves, peeled and finely sliced

20 sage leaves

850 g (1 lb, 14 oz) Roseval or similar yellow waxy potatoes, peeled

225 ml (7.1/2 fl oz) double cream

sea salt and freshly ground black pepper

Parmesan, freshly grated

Preheat the oven to 190°C/375°F/Gas 5.

Heat the oil in a frying pan and fry the pancetta over a medium heat. Stir in the garlic, add the sage, cook for a minute and remove from the heat.

Slice each potato lengthways down the middle so that you are left with two thick slices. Place in a large bowl and add the pancetta and oil mixture and the cream. Season with salt and pepper, and toss together.

Put in a baking dish, making sure that the potato, pancetta and sage are evenly distributed, cover with foil and cook in the oven for 40 minutes. About 20 minutes before the end of cooking, remove the foil so that the surface of the potatoes becomes brown. Add a little Parmesan 5 minutes before the end.

Cannellini

On a visit to Capezzana, the estate that produces our olive oil, we were told to always put bicarbonate of soda in dried pulse soaking water. This softens the skins.

Serves 6

250 g (9 oz) dried or fresh cannellini beans

2 tablespoons of bicarbonate of soda

1 large tomato

1/2 bulb garlic, unpeeled

a handful of fresh sage leaves

2 tablespoons red wine vinegar or lemon juice

6 tablespoons extra virgin olive oil

2 garlic cloves, peeled and crushed with a little salt (optional)

sea salt and freshly ground black pepper

Soak the beans in a generous amount of water overnight with the bicarbonate of soda. Drain the beans well, place in a saucepan, cover with fresh cold water and bring to the boil. Simmer for 10 minutes, then drain again. Pour in enough fresh water to cover by about 5 cm (2 in), then add the tomato, garlic bulb and sage. Return to the boil and simmer, covered, occasionally removing any scum that comes to the surface, until tender, which can vary from 40 minutes to 1.1/2 hours. Keep the beans in the water they cooked in.

To serve, drain, and dress with a mixture of the vinegar or lemon juice, oil, garlic (if using) and some salt and pepper.

Variations

Fave (dried broad beans), chickpeas and borlotti beans can all be cooked using the same method.

Lenticchie

These small and delicate organic lentils need no soaking

Serves 6

225 g (8 oz) lentilles du Puy or Castelluccio lentils

1/2 bulb garlic, cut horizontally

3 tablespoons extra virgin olive oil

juice of 1 lemon

2-3 tablespoons chopped herbs (oregano, basil, summer savory, mint or marjoram)

sea salt and freshly ground black pepper

Wash the lentils and place in a large saucepan. Cover with plenty of cold water, add the garlic and bring to the boil. Simmer very gently for about 20 minutes or until the lentils are al dente. Drain, discarding the garlic and toss the lentils in the olive oil and lemon juice. Stir in the herbs and season to taste with salt and black pepper. Serve warm.

Inzimino di Ceci
Chickpeas with Swiss Chard

Serves 6-8

175 g (6 oz) dried chickpeas soaked overnight as on page 170

1 large garlic clove, peeled

6 tablespoons olive oil

900 g (2 lb) Swiss chard leaves, washed, large stems removed

sea salt and freshly ground black pepper

1 medium red onion, peeled and coarsely chopped

2 medium carrots, peeled and cut into small pieces

2 dried chillies, crumbled

250 ml (8 fl oz) white wine

2 tablespoons Tomato Sauce (see page 273)

3 handfuls flat-leaf parsley

2 tablespoons lemon juice

extra virgin olive oil

Drain the chickpeas and place in a saucepan with water to cover, add the garlic, and 1 tablespoon of the olive oil. Bring to the boil, then simmer for 45 minutes or until tender. Keep in their liquid until ready to use. Blanch the chard and chop coarsely.

Heat the remaining olive oil in a large pan over medium heat, add the onion and carrot, and cook slowly for 15 minutes, or until the carrots are tender. Season with salt, pepper and the chilli. Pour in the wine and reduce almost completely. Add the tomato sauce and reduce until very thick. Add the chard and chickpeas and mix. Season and cook for 10 minutes. Chop two-thirds of the parsley leaves, and add to the mixture with the lemon juice. Serve sprinkled with the whole parsley leaves and a little extra virgin olive oil.

Patate al Forno con Aceto Balsamico e Timo
Potatoes Baked with Balsamic Vinegar and Thyme

Serves 6

1.3 kg (3 lb) Roseval, or similar yellow waxy potatoes, peeled

675 g (1.1/2 lb) red onions

225 g (8 oz) butter

sea salt and freshly ground black pepper

1 large bunch fresh thyme

150-175 g (5-6 oz) balsamic vinegar

Preheat the oven to 200°C/400°F/Gas 6.

Slice the potatoes lengthways to a thickness of about 1 cm (1/2 in). Trim the root ends of the onions taking care not to cut them off completely (you want the eventual slices to be held together by the root ends) and cut off the other ends. Cut the onions in half vertically, then into eighths. The onions should be the same thickness as the potatoes.

Melt the butter in a large ovenproof dish or frying pan and add the onions and potatoes. Fry, shaking and turning, so they become well coated with the butter and have taken on a little colour, about 10-15 minutes. Season with salt and pepper, add the thyme and stir in half the balsamic vinegar.

Cover the pan with foil and bake in the preheated oven for 20 minutes. Remove the foil, and stir in the remaining balsamic. Bake for another 20-30 minutes. The potatoes should take on the colour of the vinegar, and will become crisp, as will the thyme.

Mashed Potatoes with Olive Oil and Parmesan

Use yellow waxy potatoes such as Roseval, Ratte or Charlotte.

Serves 6

1.3 kg (3 lb) yellow waxy potatoes, peeled

sea salt and freshly ground black pepper

100 g (4 oz) Parmesan, freshly grated

150 ml (5 fl oz) extra virgin olive oil

Cook the potatoes in a generous amount of boiling salted water until easily pierced with a fork. Drain and mash with a fork, potato masher or whisk. Add the Parmesan, olive oil, black pepper and some more salt if necessary.

Smashed Celeriac

Serves 6

1.3 kg (3 lb) celeriac, peeled and cubed

4 tablespoons olive oil

3 garlic cloves, peeled and finely chopped

2 fresh red chillies, seeded and finely chopped (optional)

a handful of fresh thyme leaves

425 ml (15 fl oz) Chicken Stock (see page 54)

sea salt and freshly ground black pepper

Heat the oil in a heavy-bottomed saucepan and cook the garlic until light brown. Add the chilli, thyme and celeriac and cook for a few minutes to allow the flavours to combine. Pour in about 250 ml (8 fl oz) of the Chicken Stock then let it simmer, adding more as the stock is absorbed until the celeriac is soft. Mash coarsely with a whisk, and season with salt and pepper.

Finocchio alla Parmigiana
Fennel and Parmesan Gratin

Serves 6

10 fennel bulbs, trimmed

sea salt and freshly ground black pepper

300 ml (10 fl oz) double cream

50 g (2 oz) Parmesan, freshly grated

2 garlic cloves, peeled and finely chopped

Preheat the oven to 200°C/400°F/Gas 6.

Cut the fennel bulbs into six lengthways so that the individual pieces are held together by the central core. Blanch then drain well.

Toss the fennel in a mixture of the cream, half the Parmesan and the garlic. Season with salt and pepper. Put in a shallow baking dish, scatter the remaining Parmesan on top, cover with foil, and place in the preheated oven. After 20 minutes, remove the foil, then put the dish back in the oven for a further 10 minutes.

Finocchio Cucinato
Slow-Cooked Fennel

Serves 6

10 fennel bulbs, cut into quarters

5 tablespoons olive oil

sea salt and freshly ground black pepper

6 garlic cloves, peeled

Heat the oil in a large saucepan. Add the fennel, salt and pepper and cook over a medium heat, stirring occasionally until the fennel begins to brown, about 20 minutes. Add the garlic and continue to fry until the garlic is coloured light brown. Add sufficient boiling water to come one-third up the fennel, then lower the heat. Simmer until the fennel is very soft, about a further 15 minutes. Check the liquid occasionally; add a little more water if necessary, but there should be no liquid at all when the fennel is cooked.

Pomodori e Melanzane

Serves 6

4 aubergines

sea salt and freshly grated black pepper

6 tablespoons olive oil

2 garlic cloves, peeled and finely sliced

1 x 800 g (1.3/4 lb) tin peeled plum tomatoes, drained of their juices

a handful of basil leaves, chopped

Cut the aubergines into 2.5 cm (1 in) cubes, sprinkle with salt, and leave in a colander to drain for 30 minutes to get rid of the bitter juices. Rinse and dry well on kitchen paper.

Heat half the olive oil in a large saucepan and fry the garlic until light brown. Add the tomatoes and simmer for at least 40 minutes until very thick.

In a separate large pan heat the rest of the olive oil until it is almost smoking. Add the aubergine in batches and fry until brown on all sides. Remove the aubergine using a slotted spoon, and add to the warm tomato sauce. Season and stir in the basil. Serve at room temperature.

Melanzane al Funghetto

Serves 6

4 aubergines

sea salt and freshly ground black pepper

6 tablespoons olive oil

2 garlic cloves, peeled and sliced

6 salted anchovy fillets, prepared (see page 304)

3 tablespoons chopped flat-leaf parsley

2 dessertspoons salted capers, prepared (see page 306)

Cut the aubergines into 2.5 cm (1 in) cubes, sprinkle with salt and drain in a colander for 30 minutes to get rid of the bitter juices. Rinse and dry well.

In a large heavy saucepan heat half the oil until almost smoking. Fry the aubergine in batches, until brown on all sides. Remove from the pan using a slotted spoon, and drain.

In a clean saucepan, gently fry the garlic in the remaining oil until it starts to colour, then add the anchovies. Stir for 1 minute, breaking the anchovies into the oil. Add the parsley and the capers. Return the aubergine to the pan, season and serve.

Cicoria al Forno
Baked Chicory

Serves 6

6 heads chicory, red or white

50 g (2 oz) butter

100 g (4 oz) slices pancetta affumicata, finely chopped

50 g (2 oz) fresh breadcrumbs

finely grated zest and juice of 2 lemons

3 tablespoons chopped flat-leaf parsley

100 g (4 oz) Parmesan, freshly grated

sea salt and freshly ground black pepper

250 ml (8 fl oz) double cream

Preheat the oven to 190°C/375°F/Gas 5, and use some of the butter to grease the inside of a shallow ovenproof dish.

Slice the chicory lengthways into quarters, and layer in the dish at a slight angle, cut side up and overlapping.

Mix the pancetta with the breadcrumbs, lemon zest, parsley and half the Parmesan, and season with salt and pepper. Scatter over the chicory, pour over the lemon juice, and dot with the remaining butter. Cover with foil and place in the preheated oven. After 40 minutes, remove the foil, pour over the cream, sprinkle with the remaining Parmesan, and return the dish to the oven for another 15-20 minutes until the cream has thickened.

Funghi Brasati
Braised Field and Wild Mushrooms

Serves 6

100 g (4 oz) dried porcini mushrooms, reconstituted (see page 312)

675 g (1.1/2 lb) medium flat field mushrooms, thickly sliced

5 tablespoons olive oil

3 garlic cloves, peeled and sliced

sea salt and freshly ground black pepper

2 tablespoons chopped basil, marjoram or flat-leaf parsley

juice of 1 lemon

Heat 4 tablespoons of the olive oil in a large heavy-bottomed pan until smoking. Add the sliced fresh mushrooms and fry, stirring constantly, for 15-20 minutes, or until the mushrooms have become very dark and soft. Remove and keep warm.

Wipe clean the pan. Strain the porcini, retaining their juices, and rinse and squeeze dry. Heat the remaining olive oil in the pan and gently fry the garlic and porcini. When the garlic begins to colour, pour the strained porcini juices into the pan and simmer until reduced to 2 tablespoons. Add the cooked mushrooms, season with salt and pepper, and stir to combine the flavours. Add the herbs and lemon juice and serve.

Braised Trompettes de Mort

Unlike other mushrooms, these do not absorb water, so they can be washed like salad leaves.

Serves 6

700 g (1.1/2 lb trompettes de mort

4 tablespoons olive oil

3 garlic cloves, peeled and cut into thin slices

a handful of flat-leaf parsley, finely chopped

sea salt and freshly ground black pepper

Cut off the stalk end of each mushroom and wash and dry in a salad spinner.

Heat 3 tablespoons of the oil in a large heavy-bottomed saucepan and when very hot add the mushrooms, turning to cook quickly. Remove from the pan, and drain, retaining the juices. Add the remaining oil to the pan with the slivers of garlic and fry until light brown; add a little of the mushroom juice, the parsley and the mushrooms. Turn once, season with salt and pepper, and serve immediately.

Fagiolini alla Parmigiana
Green Beans with Parmesan

Serves 6

450 g (1 lb) French beans, trimmed

sea salt and freshly ground black pepper

100 g (4 oz) unsalted butter

100 g (4 oz) Parmesan, freshly grated

In a saucepan with a lid, bring roughly 2 litres (3.1/2 pints) of water to the boil with a dessertspoon of salt.

Put the green beans into the water and cover until the water comes back to the boil, then remove the lid and cook until al dente.

Drain the beans and return to the saucepan with the butter. Season with pepper and stir in the Parmesan. Keep over the heat until the Parmesan begins to go stringy and coats the beans. Serve immediately.

Braised Cavolo Nero

Serves 6

> 6 heads cavolo nero
>
> sea salt and freshly ground black pepper
>
> 3 tablespoons olive oil
>
> 2 garlic cloves, peeled and finely sliced
>
> extra virgin olive oil

Remove the tough centre stems from the cavolo nero leaves. Wash and blanch in boiling salted water for about 3 minutes. It is important not to overcook.

Heat the olive oil in a heavy-bottomed saucepan and gently fry the garlic. When it begins to colour, add the blanched cavolo, and season generously. Cook together to blend the garlic with the cavolo, about 5 minutes. Remove from the heat, pour over extra virgin olive oil and serve.

Spinach with Oil and Lemon

Serves 6

> 900 g (2 lb) spinach, washed and tough stalks removed
>
> 3 tablespoons extra virgin olive oil
>
> sea salt and freshly ground black pepper
>
> juice of 1/2 lemon

Heat the oil in a large saucepan with a lid. Put the wet spinach into the oil, season with salt and pepper, stir once and cover tightly with the lid for about a minute. Squeeze over the lemon juice and serve.

Carrots Dada

This is best made with mature organic carrots, usually available at the end of summer, early autumn.

Serves 6

1.5 kg (3.1/4 lb) carrots

2 garlic bulbs with large cloves, peeled

350 ml (12 fl oz) olive oil

sea salt and coarsely ground black pepper

Trim and wash the carrots, and slice them diagonally into slices about 3 mm (1/8 in) thick. Slice the garlic cloves in half.

In a large heavy-bottomed saucepan, heat about 50-85 ml (2-3 fl oz) of the olive oil or enough to completely cover the base of the pan. When hot, add one layer only of carrot slices – you will be cooking in batches. Fry gently, turning each piece over as it begins to brown. As you turn, season with salt and pepper, and add a proportion – about 2 tablespoons – of the garlic slices. As the garlic and carrots brown, remove using a slotted spoon.

Add a further batch of carrots to the oil and cook in the same way. Add more oil only when the carrots have absorbed what is in the pan.

These carrots have a caramelised appearance, and remain separate. The thick pieces of garlic should remain distinct.

Sformato di Spinaci
Baked Spinach

Serves 6

1.3 kg (3 lb) spinach, tough stalks removed

2 eggs

400 ml (14 fl oz) double cream

100 g (4 oz) Parmesan, freshly grated

1/2 teaspoon grated nutmeg

sea salt and freshly ground black pepper

Preheat the oven to 190°C/375°F/Gas 5.

Beat the eggs and cream together for a minute in a large bowl. Add the Parmesan, nutmeg, pepper and a little salt.

Blanch the spinach in plenty of boiling salted water for 1 minute, and drain well. Chop roughly and mix well with the egg and cream mixture. Pour into a medium-sized baking dish: the mixture should not be less than 4 cm (1.1/2 in) deep. Place uncovered in the top of the preheated oven for 30 minutes.

Serve hot. The top should be crisp, while the underneath should still be slightly creamy.

Fish
Shel

and

lfish

5

When the fish is delivered to the River Cafe, it is checked carefully. The flesh must be rigid when prodded with a finger, the skin shiny and firm, the scales intact, the gills a deep red colour and the eyes clear.

Then we decide on the cooking method. We prefer to cook the fish whole – usually grilled.

If the fish is too large, we cut it into fillets and cook it according to season and the type of fish. We might stud sea bass with summer herbs before grilling, wrap a red mullet in leaves of red trevise and seal it – airtight – in silver foil before baking, or pan fry and then bake monkfish with pancetta.

Char-grilled squid is simple and delicious. The prepared squid is placed on the hottest part of the char-grill for one second only, and it is then served with a generous piece of lemon and rocket. This was one of the first fish dishes we created and it has been on the menu almost every day since we opened.

We have included two recipes for fish stews. Italian fish stews reflect the regional quality of the country's cooking. Regions are competitive about their stews and are proud of their own version. Venice has its Broeto, to which little is added to alter the taste of the fish, while the Livornese include many more varieties of local fish and add chilli and garlic.

Branzino ai Ferri
Grilled Sea Bass Fillets

Serves 6

1 x 2.7 – 3.5 kg (6-8 lb) sea bass

1 tablespoon olive oil

sea salt and freshly ground black pepper

3 lemons

Prepare the sea bass by snipping off the side and back fins with a strong pair of scissors. With a fish scaler or large strong knife, scrape off the scales. This is best done by holding the fish by the tail in a sink and scraping downwards. It is essential to do this thoroughly. Gut the fish by running a sharp knife up from the base of the belly to the head. Remove the guts and wash the fish well.

To cut into fillets, lie the fish on its side and, using a sharp filleting knife, carefully slice along the backbone, from tail to head, keeping close to the bones with the blade so as not to waste any flesh. Then cut downwards around the head, which will enable you to remove the fillet. Repeat this with the other side of the fish.

Place the fillets skin side down and run your hand over them to check for any bones. Pull out any that remain using tweezers. Cut each fillet into three equal portions.

Lightly brush the pieces of fish with oil, season well with salt and pepper and grill for 3 minutes on each side, or until cooked.

Serve with lemon.

Branzino al Cartoccio
Baked Sea Bass

The foil packages should be opened at the table to appreciate the smell of the steamed fish and mushrooms.

Serves 6

1 x 2.7 – 3.5 kg (6-8 lb) sea bass, scaled and cleaned (see page 192)

20 g (3/4 oz) dried porcini, reconstituted (see page 312)

olive oil

sea salt and freshly ground black pepper

a few large sprigs of fresh thyme

100g (4oz) soft butter

Fillet the bass as described in the previous recipe.

Drain the porcini, retaining their soaking water, wash and dry. Fry them in a tablespoon of the olive oil for a few minutes, then add some of the carefully strained soaking water. Season and cook together for a few minutes until soft.

Preheat the oven to 200-230°C/400-450°F/Gas 6-8.

Make six rectangles of doubled foil, dull side out, brush with oil and sprinkle with salt and pepper. Place a fillet in the middle of one half of each piece of foil, skin side down, and put a few porcini, a couple of small thyme sprigs and a knob of butter on top. Moisten with a little of the porcini juices. Fold the other half of the foil over and seal the edges, to make a loose but airtight package.

Place the packages on a baking tray and bake in the oven for 10-12 minutes. The foil will puff up. Remove from the oven and rest for about 2 minutes before serving.

Variation Instead of dried porcini and tomatoes, use sun-dried tomatoes and trevise leaves, and add a tablespoon of olive oil to each package.

Branzino Arrosto
Roasted Marinated Sea Bass

The grilling of the skin before baking gives the bass a distinctive and interesting flavour

Serves 4-6

1 x 2.25 kg (5 lb) sea bass, scaled and cleaned but not filleted (see page 192)

2 tablespoons fennel seeds

sea salt and coarsely ground black pepper

2 red onions, peeled and sliced thinly

2 lemons, sliced

a few parsley stalks

2 fresh fennel bulbs, trimmed and sliced

juice of 1 lemon

5 tablespoons olive oil

75 ml (2.1/2 fl oz) white wine

Preheat the oven to 190°C/375°F/Gas 5. Preheat the grill.

Put half the fennel seeds and some salt and pepper inside the cavity of the fish, brush the skin with a little olive oil and grill for about 5-6 minutes on each side until the skin is lightly charred.

Place half the onion and lemon slices, parsley stalks, fennel slices and the remaining fennel seeds in a large ovenproof dish, lay the fish on top and cover with the remaining onion, lemon, parsley and fennel. Pour over the lemon juice, olive oil and white wine, and bake in the oven for about 30 minutes, or until the flesh is firm to the touch.

Serve either hot or cold with Salsa Verde (see page 270).

Branzino al Sale
Sea Bass Baked in Salt

Wild salmon can be prepared and cooked in the same way.

Serves 6

1 x 1.8 kg (4 lb) sea bass, scaled and cleaned, but not filleted (see page 192)

1 lemon, sliced

1 small handful dried fennel stalks

3.6 kg (8 lb) coarse preserving salt

100 g (4 oz) plain flour

Preheat the oven to 200°C/400°F/Gas 6.

Put the lemon and dried fennel stalks inside the cavity of the fish. Cover the bottom of the baking dish with half the salt and lay the fish on top. Cover the fish completely with the remaining salt.

Mix the flour into a thin paste with a little water. Brush the surface of the salt evenly with the flour solution.

Bake the fish in the preheated oven. After 20 minutes, insert a skewer into the fish. If the tip of the skewer is very hot, the fish is ready.

Crack open the salt crust and remove the hard pieces, ensuring that no salt remains on the flesh of the fish. Carefully lift the fish and place on a platter. Remove the skin.

Serve warm with Salsa Verde, Aioli or Basil Mayonnaise (see pages 270 and 272).

Baccalà alla Griglia
Grilled Salt Cod

Serves 6

6 pieces salt cod, about 350 g (12 oz) each, cut from the thick central parts of the fish

olive oil for brushing

crushed black pepper

2 lemons

Soak the cod in cold water for 48 hours, changing the water three to four times a day. They will plump up as they soak and release the salt.

Preheat a grill.

Take the pieces of salt cod out of the water, pat and squeeze dry with a clean cloth. It is important that they are completely dry before they are grilled. Brush with olive oil and grill on either side until the cod is no longer transparent, about 6-8 minutes.

Serve with Quick Sweet Tomato Sauce with Basil, Almond Aioli, Fresh Red Chilli Sauce, or Slow-Cooked Tomato Sauce (see pages 267, 272 and 273).

Rombo alla Griglia
Grilled Turbot

Serves 10

1 x 2.75 kg (6 lb) turbot

olive oil

sea salt and freshly ground black pepper

Wash the turbot in cold water. Using a sharp filleting knife with a long flexible blade, slice down the central spine of the fish from head to tail. This central spine can be found by running your finger along the fish to feel for it.

Depending on which side of the spine your knife falls, proceed to fillet that portion of the fish. This is best done by starting at the head end. Cut along the edge where it meets the body, and then down the length of the spine, slowly easing the flesh away from the bone. Continue to do this until the fillet is released from the bones. Trim the edges of the fillets, removing any bones.

Two of the four fillets will be smaller than the others. Cut these smaller fillets in half. The larger fillets should be cut evenly into three. Brush the flesh side of the fillets with oil, season with salt and pepper, and grill, for 3-4 minutes on each side, or until cooked.

Triglia ai Ferri
Grilled Red Mullet

Serves 6

6 x 300-350 g (10-12 oz) red mullet

sea salt and freshly ground black pepper

Prepare the red mullet by snipping off the back and side fins with a pair of strong scissors. Then remove the scales by wiping them off with your hands under fast running water. When all of the scales have been removed, stick a sharp knife into the base of the belly of the fish and then slit upwards towards the head. Under more cold running water, remove the guts and any congealed blood along the spine, carefully retaining the livers. Give the fish a final rinse and dry thoroughly. Season.

Place the mullet on a hot grill and grill for 4-5 minutes on each side or until cooked.

Serve with Anchovy and Rosemary Sauce or Salsa Verde (see pages 266 and 270).

Acciughe Fresche Marinate
Marinated Fresh Anchovies

This recipe should only be prepared with really fresh large anchovies.

Serves 6

2 kg (4.1/2 lb) fresh anchovies

sea salt and freshly ground black pepper

2 tablespoons dried chilli, crumbled

1 bunch fresh flat-leaf parsley, finely chopped

juice of 4 lemons

250 ml (8 fl oz) extra virgin olive oil

Fillet the anchovies by pulling the head and spine away from the fish, then cut off the tails and fins. You will have two fillets from each fish.

In a serving dish arrange a layer of anchovies side by side, not overlapping, and sprinkle with a little sea salt, black pepper, chilli and parsley. Pour over a generous amount of lemon juice – this is what 'cooks' the anchovies – and some olive oil. Repeat the layers, making sure that the top layer is covered with oil and lemon.

Leave to marinate for about 2 hours before serving with either salad or bruschetta.

Coda di Rospo in Cartoccio
Baked Monkfish with Crème Fraîche in Foil

Serves 6

6 x 200 g (7 oz) pieces monkfish fillet

2 tablespoons fresh rosemary

3 garlic cloves, peeled and cut into slivers

100g (4oz) butter, melted

sea salt and freshly ground black pepper

6 dessertspoons crème fraîche

6 dessertspoons extra dry white vermouth

Preheat the oven to 200°C/400°F/Gas 6.

With a sharp knife, make tiny slits evenly all over the monkfish, and insert 2-3 rosemary leaves, a sliver of garlic, and some salt and pepper halfway into each.

Make six rectangles of doubled foil, dull side out. Brush with butter and place a piece of monkfish in the centre of one half of the foil. Put a dessertspoon of crème fraîche on top. Fold the other half of the foil over the monkfish, and then fold the sides in tightly, but leave the top open. Pour a dessertspoon of vermouth into each 'parcel' and seal well. It is essential for the package to be airtight to stop the steam escaping.

Place the foil packages on a baking tray, and bake at the top of the preheated oven for 20 minutes. Serve immediately with the juices.

Triglia al Cartoccio con Treviso
Red Mullet Wrapped in Trevise

Serves 6

6 x 300-350 g (10-12 oz) red mullet, scaled and cleaned (see page 192)

6 small heads trevise or 24 radicchio leaves, washed and dried

75 g (3 oz) butter

2 garlic cloves, peeled and cut into fine slivers

200 g (7 oz) fresh porcini mushrooms, brushed clean and sliced

sea salt and freshly ground black pepper

olive oil

6 sprigs fresh thyme

3 lemons

Preheat the oven to 230°C/450°F/Gas 8.

Heat the butter in a pan, and fry the garlic until light brown. Add the sliced porcini, and season with salt and pepper.

Make six rectangles of doubled foil, dull side out, and brush with oil. Place three or four trevise leaves in the centre of one half of each piece of foil and add two slices of porcini, a little of the melted butter and some salt and pepper. Place the mullet on top, with a sprig of thyme inside. Put some more porcini slices on top, with a few extra trevise leaves, and a little more melted butter. Fold the other half of the foil over and seal the edges, to make a loose, but leakproof, package.

Place the packages on a baking tray and bake in the oven for 10-15 minutes. Remove the mullet from the foil and serve with lemon quarters.

Mazzancolle ai Ferri
Grilled Langoustine with Fennel and Chilli Sauce

Serves 6

5-6 medium langoustines (or tiger prawns) per person

lemon quarters

For the sauce

the green herb tops of 4 fennel bulbs, or a handful of fresh fennel herb

1 fennel bulb

3 fresh red chillies, seeded and finely chopped

juice of 1 lemon

5 tablespoons extra virgin olive oil

sea salt and freshly ground black pepper

Preheat a grill to very hot.

Finely chop the green fennel tops and the fennel bulb and put, together with the chopped chilli, in a bowl. Add the lemon juice and leave for 5-10 minutes. Add the olive oil and season with salt and pepper.

Grill the langoustines or prawns for 2-3 minutes on either side.

Serve with lemon quarters and the sauce. A basil mayonnaise (see page 272) is a good alternative.

Calamari ai Ferri con Peperoncini
Grilled Squid with Chillies

Serves 6

6 medium squid, no bigger than your hand

For the sauce

12 large fresh red chillies, seeded and very finely chopped

extra virgin olive oil

sea salt and freshly ground black pepper

To serve

8 tablespoons Oil and Lemon Dressing (see page 166)

225 g (8 oz) rocket leaves

3 lemons

Clean the squid by cutting the body open to make a flat piece. Scrape out the guts, keeping the tentacles in their bunches but removing the eyes and mouth.

Using a serrated knife, score the inner side of the flattened squid body with parallel lines 1 cm (1/2 in) apart, and then equally apart the other way to make cross-hatching.

To make the sauce, put the chopped chilli in a bowl and cover with about 2.5 cm (1 in) of the oil. Season with salt and pepper.

Place the squid (including the tentacles) scored side down on a very hot grill, season with salt and pepper and grill for 1-2 minutes. Turn the squid pieces over; they will immediately curl up, by which time they will be cooked.

Toss the rocket in the Oil and Lemon Dressing. Arrange a squid body and tentacles on each plate with some of the rocket. Place a little of the chilli on the squid and serve with lemon quarters.

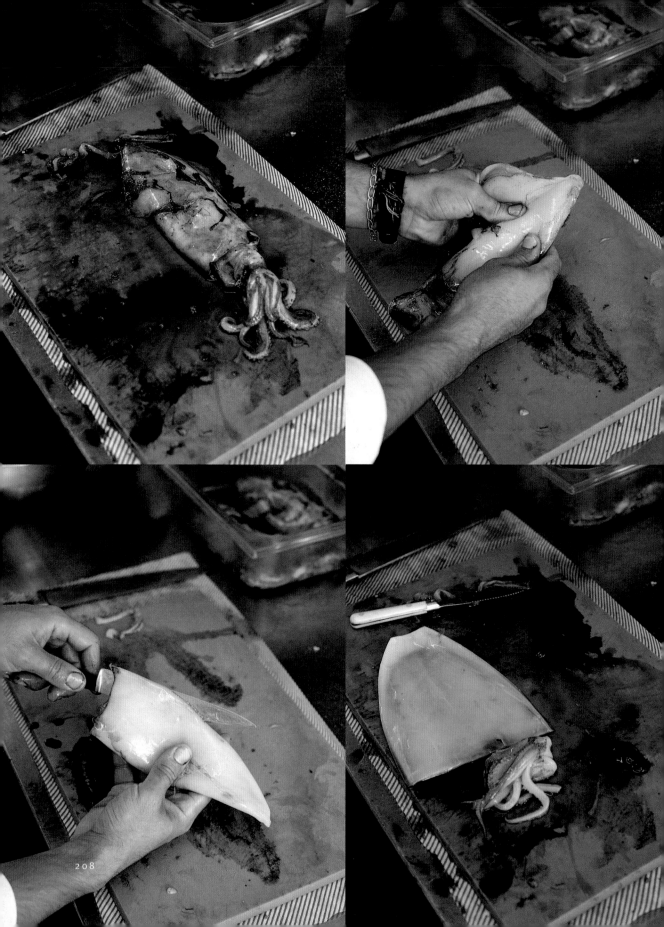

Caposante in Padella con Capperi
Pan-Fried Scallops with Capers

To grill scallops, prepare as below. Lightly brush with oil and season. Grill on a medium hot grill for a few minutes on each side, and serve with lemon quarters.

Serves 6

18 medium scallops

olive oil

sea salt and freshly ground black pepper

3 tablespoons salted capers, prepared (see page 306)

1 bunch sage leaves, stalks removed

1 lemon

Prepare the scallops by placing them flat shell side down on a board. Insert a sharp 13 cm (5 in) knife close to the hinge of the shell, and prise open. Keeping the blade of the knife flat against the shell bottom so as to avoid cutting into the scallop, gently using a sawing motion, remove the scallop from the bottom shell. The scallop shell should now be open with the scallop nestling in the top curved half of the shell. With a spoon carefully scoop out the scallop. Trim the membrane and dirty end of the coral and wash the scallop in cold water. Pat dry.

Brush a frying pan with a little oil, to prevent the scallops sticking, and place over a high heat. When smoking, add the scallops, season with a little salt and pepper, and cook for 2 minutes on one side. Turn the scallops over and immediately add the capers and sage leaves, plus a little extra oil so that the sage leaves fry. Cook for a further 2 minutes, shaking the pan constantly. Squeeze in the juice of the lemon and serve.

eat

6

In Italian kitchens the oven is rarely used for cooking meat and at the River Cafe we too either pot roast our meats on top of the stove, pan fry, or grill them. The notable exception is the classic Bollito Misto.

Although grilling is now considered the modern healthy way to cook meat, it is a very traditional Tuscan method. A first course of pasta or bread soup, will often be followed by grilled pork, lamb or steak served somewhat austerely with a piece of lemon. Meat used for grilling must be of the best quality, full of flavour and tender. Sealing first over or under an intense heat will keep it tender and moist.

The method of slow cooking meats on top of the stove, not surprisingly, originates in the colder northern regions such as Piedmont. In the winter we cook such dishes as Beef in Tegame, Lo Shinco, or Maiale in Latte.

Bollito Misto is one of our favourite recipes. The meats – ox tongue, shin of beef, cotechino sausage and a boiling hen – are cooked separately in different broths with herbs and tomatoes and when the meats are carved, the seasoned broth is ladled over. Lentils or cannelli beans are served with the bollito and salsa verde and mostarda di cremona are passed around the table. Wonderful ingredients, straightforward and uncomplicated cooking yet subtle tastes – this is the essence of Bollito Misto and of Italian cooking.

Ossobuco in Bianco

This recipe is different from the traditional ossobuco as it omits tomatoes and includes anchovies. As pieces of ossobuco vary in size, you may need more than one each. If you have some left over it is delicious eaten cold.

Serves 6

8 x 5 cm (2 in) pieces of veal shin

75 g (3 oz) plain flour

sea salt and freshly ground black pepper

115 g (4 oz) butter

2 tablespoons olive oil

2 small red onions, peeled and finely chopped

4 celery stalks, trimmed and finely chopped

2 garlic cloves, peeled and chopped

9 salted anchovies, prepared (see page 304)

1/2 bottle dry white wine

For the gremolata

finely grated zest of 2 lemons

1 garlic clove, peeled and very finely chopped

3 tablespoons chopped flat-leaf parsley

Preheat the oven to 150°C/300°F/Gas 2.

Dust each piece of ossobuco with flour, salt and pepper. In a large heavy-bottomed casserole, just large enough to hold all the pieces of ossobuco in one layer, melt half the butter and all the oil and brown and seal the ossobuco on each side. Remove from the pan and pour away the fat. Then add the remaining butter, and gently fry the onion and celery until very soft but not brown. Then add the garlic and anchovies and mash until the anchovies have melted, this will only take a second. Pour in the wine, bring to the boil and reduce.

Carefully put the ossobuco back into the casserole, making sure that the bones are placed so that the marrow cannot fall out during the cooking. Cover with greaseproof paper and the lid, and cook in the preheated oven for at least 2.1/2 hours.

Mix together the gremolata ingredients and sprinkle over each ossobuco. This is classically served with Risotto Milanese (see page 100).

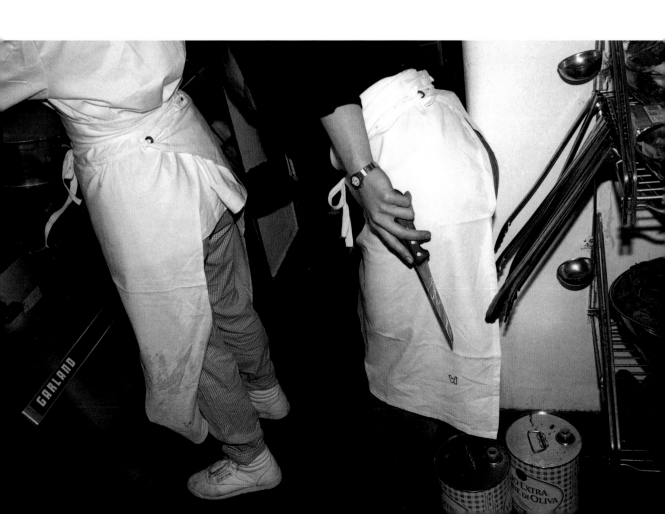

Shinco Arrosto
Roast Whole Shin of Veal

In this recipe the shin of veal is cooked whole, slowly, on top of the stove, until the meat becomes so soft and gelatinous that it falls away from the bone.

Serves 8

2 shins of veal, cut at each end, exposing the marrow

2 tablespoons olive oil

sea salt and freshly ground black pepper

1 head celery, finely chopped

2 red onions, peeled and finely chopped

1 tablespoon fresh thyme leaves

300 ml (10 fl oz) dry white wine

1 x 400 g (14 oz) tin peeled plum tomatoes

300 ml (10 fl oz) Chicken or Veal Stock (see pages 54 and 55)

12 small carrots, trimmed

Gremolata (see page 216)

In a large heavy saucepan heat the oil and brown the veal shins on all sides. Season, and remove from the pan.

Add the celery and onion to the pan, and cook until soft but not brown, about 15 minutes. Add the thyme and cook for a further 5 minutes. Raise the heat, pour in the white wine, the plum tomatoes and stock, and bring to the boil. Lower the heat to a simmer, and return the shins of veal to the pan. Cover with greaseproof paper and the lid and cook gently for 2 hours.

About 10 minutes before serving, add the carrots. Carve the meat into medium thick slices and serve with the juices from the pan. Knock the shin bone to release the marrow and add a spoonful to each portion. Sprinkle with gremolata.

Vitello Arrosto con Salvia
Veal Loin Roasted with Sage

Serves 6

1.8 – 2.3 kg (4-5 lb) boned loin of veal, skin and most of the fat removed

sea salt and freshly ground black pepper

20 sage leaves, finely chopped

2 teaspoons finely chopped rosemary leaves

100 g (4 oz) unsalted butter

3 garlic cloves, peeled and sliced

75 g (3 oz) dried porcini mushrooms, reconstituted (see page 312)

250 ml (8 fl oz) dry white wine

Season the meat with salt and pepper, and rub the rosemary and sage all over.

In a heavy-bottomed casserole, just large enough to hold the veal, melt half the butter. When foaming, add the veal and brown on all sides. Pour away the fat. Add 15g (1/2 oz) of the butter, the garlic and the porcini, and fry briefly. Add some of the porcini soaking water to deglaze the pan. This must be done over a high heat. Add the white wine and reduce the heat.

Return the veal to the casserole, and put the remaining butter on top. Cover with a piece of greaseproof paper and then the lid, slightly askew. Cook on top of the stove for about 45 minutes on a very gentle heat, or in a preheated oven at about 150°C/300°F/Gas 2.

Slice and serve with the juices from the pan.

Costolette di Vitello
Grilled Veal Chops

A paste of sage, lemon peel and prosciutto fat enhances a simple veal chop.

Serves 4

4 thick veal chops

50 g (2 oz) prosciutto fat

peelof 2 lemons

2 tablespoons sage leaves

1 tablespoon lemon juice

sea salt and freshly ground black pepper

Put the prosciutto fat, lemon peel, sage leaves, lemon juice and a seasoning of salt and pepper in a food processor and pulse-chop to make a coarse, thick paste.

Dry the veal chops thoroughly and spread the mixture evenly on each side.

Grill for 5-8 minutes on each side.

Shinco di Agnello
Slow-Cooked Lamb Shanks

Serves 6

6 small lamb shanks

plain flour for dusting

sea salt and freshly ground black pepper

2 tablespoons olive oil

6 red onions, peeled and finely sliced

a handful of chopped rosemary leaves

4 garlic cloves, peeled and chopped

175 ml (6 fl oz) balsamic vinegar

300 ml (10 fl oz) red wine

Preheat the oven to 200°C/400°F/Gas 6 (or you can cook on top of the stove).

Dust the lamb shanks with seasoned flour.

In a heavy-bottomed saucepan with a lid, heat the oil and brown the shanks on all sides then remove. Lower the heat, add the onions and cook for about 10-15 minutes until light brown. Add the rosemary and garlic and cook for another couple of minutes. Raise the heat and add the balsamic vinegar and the wine. Reduce for a couple of minutes.

Return the shanks to the pan, reduce the heat and cover with a piece of moistened greaseproof paper and the lid. Cook in the oven for about 2-2.1/2 hours, or alternatively on top of the stove.

Check the shanks from time to time, basting with the juices or adding more wine if they look too dry. Serve whole, with the juices.

Maiale al Latte
Pork Cooked in Milk

The curdle that results from the slow cooking together of lemon and milk makes a delicious sauce

Serves 6

1 x 1.8 – 2.25 kg (4-5 lb) boned loin of young organic pork, rind and most of the fat removed

sea salt and freshly ground black pepper

2 tablespoons olive oil

50 g (2 oz) butter

5 garlic cloves, peeled and halved

a small handful of fresh sage leaves (optional)

1.5 litres (2.1/2 pints) milk

pared rind of 2 lemons, pith removed

Generously season the pork on all sides. Heat the olive oil in a heavy-bottomed saucepan with a lid just large enough to hold the pork. Brown the meat on all sides, then remove. Pour away the fat.

Melt the butter in the pan, add the garlic with the sage leaves (if using) and, before the garlic begins to colour, return the pork to the pan. Add enough hot milk to come three-quarters of the way up the pork. Bring to the boil, add the lemon rind and reduce the heat. Place the lid on the pan, slightly askew, and very slowly simmer for about 1.1/2-2 hours. Resist the temptation to disturb the meat.

When the pork is cooked, the milk will have curdled into brown nuggets. Carefully move the meat, slice quickly and spoon over the sauce.

Brasato di Maiale con Aceto
Pork Braised with Vinegar

Serves 6

1 x 1.8 – 2.25 kg (4-5 lb) boned loin of young organic pork, rind and most of the fat removed

sea salt

2 tablespoons olive oil

150 ml (5 fl oz) red wine vinegar

150 ml (5 fl oz) Chianti Classico

1 tablespoon black peppercorns

12 fresh bay leaves

Generously season the pork with salt.

In a heavy saucepan with a lid, heat the olive oil and brown the meat on all sides. Remove the meat and put to one side. Lower the heat and pour the vinegar into the pan. Bring to the boil, and reduce the liquid by half. Add the wine, 100 ml (4 fl oz) water, the peppercorns and bay leaves and lower the heat to a simmer.

Return the pork to the pan and turn to coat it in the juices. Put the lid on but slightly askew. Simmer very gently for an hour, turning the meat two or three times during cooking. If the juices seem to be drying up, add a little more wine or water.

When the meat is cooked (still soft when prodded), turn off the heat, add extra salt to the juices, and let the pork relax for 5 minutes. Slice and serve with the juices and the bay leaves.

Maiale Arrosto con Aceto Balsamico
Pork Roasted with Balsamic Vinegar

In this recipe the meat is first grilled to give a burnt flavour which contrasts with that of the sweet balsamic vinegar.

Serves 6

1 x 1.8 – 2.25 kg (4-5 lb) boned loin of young organic pork, rind and most of the fat removed

sea salt and freshly ground black pepper

2 red onions, peeled and cut into eighths lengthways

100 g (4 oz) butter

1 tablespoon roughly chopped fresh rosemary

350 ml (12 fl oz) balsamic vinegar

60 ml (2 fl oz) red wine

Preheat the oven to 220°C/425°F/Gas 7.

Season the meat, then grill on all sides to seal. Ideally this should be done on a barbecue or cast-iron griddle.

Place a baking dish over a medium to low heat, soften the onion in the butter for 5 minutes, then stir in the rosemary. Add the grilled pork and half the balsamic vinegar. Turn the pork so that it is well coated, then put into the preheated oven. Roast for about 40 minutes: after the first 10 minutes turn the pork and stir the onions once; about 5 minutes before the end of cooking, add the remaining balsamic vinegar.

Put the pork on a board on one side to relax for a couple of minutes. Deglaze the juices and onion in the dish with a little wine, until a concentrated juice .

Slice the pork thinly, and serve with the juices.

Filetto di Manzo in Tegame
Braised Beef Fillet

Serves 6

1 x 1.8 kg (4 lb) fillet of beef, trimmed of all fat

6-8 garlic cloves, peeled and cut into fine slivers

100 g (4 oz) prosciutto fat, cut into similar-sized slivers

a handful of fresh rosemary leaves

sea salt and freshly ground black pepper

300 g (10 oz) coppa di Parma, sliced thinly

2 tablespoons olive oil

50 g (2 oz) butter

2 medium red onions, peeled and chopped

1/2 head celery, trimmed and chopped

1 bottle Freisa, or another red wine from Barolo

50-85 ml (2-3 fl oz) Chicken or Veal Stock, if necessary (see pages 54 and 55)

With a sharp knife, make small incisions all over the fillet following the grain of the meat. Into each incision insert a sliver each of garlic and prosciutto fat, with a few rosemary leaves and some salt and pepper.

Now carefully wrap the fillet from end to end with the coppa slices, slightly overlapping them, and tie on evenly with string, keeping the string turns close together. You may not use all the coppa, in which case cut the remainder into slivers.

In a saucepan just large enough to hold the fillet, heat the oil and butter and gently brown the wrapped fillet on all sides. Remove and set aside. Add the onion and coppa and gently fry until the onion has become light brown. Now return the fillet to the pan, and add enough wine to come halfway up the sides of the fillet. Bring to the boil, reduce the heat, and cover with a piece of moistened greaseproof paper and put on the lid, slightly askew. Simmer gently for 20-30 minutes.

Test the meat by pressing the fillet – if it gives gently to your touch, it will be rare. Remove from the pan. The sauce should be quite dense; if too thin, reduce over a fierce heat. Check for seasoning.

Untie the string, slice the fillet, and spoon over the juices. Serve with wet polenta (see page 120).

Bistecca di manzo con Rucola
Steak with Rocket

Steak hiding a rocket salad can be served the other way round, with the rocket hiding the steak!

Serves 1

1 x 225 g (8 oz) entrecote steak, all fat and sinews removed

a handful of rocket leaves, washed and dried

sea salt and freshly ground black pepper

1 lemon quarter

For the dressing

5 teaspoons extra virgin olive oil

juice of 1/2 lemon

1 tablespoon red wine vinegar

Combine the oil, lemon juice, vinegar and some salt and pepper for the dressing.

Pull out a piece of cling film six times the width of the steak. Place the steak in the centre of one-half of the cling film, and fold the other half over it. Now, gently, using either a wooden mallet or a rolling pin, beat the steak out evenly until paper thin and the size of a plate. Season on both sides.

Preheat a grill to very hot. Carefully place the steak on the grill, brush with olive oil and sear on both sides, then remove.

Dress the rocket leaves and place on warm plates. Cover completely with the steak.

Carpaccio con Salmoriglio
Beef Fillet with Salmoriglio

We char-grill the whole fillet just to form a crust adding flavour to the raw beef.

Serves 6 as a main course, 10 as a starter

1 top-quality beef fillet, about 1.5 – 1.8 kg (3.1/2-4 lb), trimmed

sea salt and freshly ground black pepper

Thyme Salmoriglio (see page 269)

1 kg (2.1/4 lb) rocket leaves

Oil and Lemon Dressing (see page 166)

Preheat a grill to very hot. Rub the fillet with salt and pepper, then briefly grill, turning continuously to blacken the outsides, but making sure that the centre remains raw.

Slice the cold fillet into 1cm (1/2in) slices on a board. Using a large pointed cooking knife, press and spread the slices to make them thin and lacy. The grilled edges will hold the pieces together. Spread out the slices on the plate, and spoon over the thyme sauce. Lightly toss the rocket leaves with the Oil and Lemon Dressing .

Agnello Marinato alla Griglia
Marinated Grilled Lamb

When we grill lamb we choose the whole leg because it has such a definite taste and texture. Only spring lamb is suitable for this method of cooking.

Serves 6

1 leg of spring lamb, about 2.25 kg (5 lb) in weight, boned and butterflied

5 garlic cloves, peeled and crushed

2 tablespoons chopped rosemary leaves

a good pinch of coarsely ground black pepper

2 tablespoons lemon juice

3 tablespoons olive oil

1 tablespoon sea salt

Mix the crushed garlic, rosemary, and pepper in a bowl, and rub into the cut side of the meat. Place the meat in a shallow dish and pour over the lemon juice and olive oil. Turn the meat over a couple of times to make sure it is coated, then cover. Leave to marinate at room temperature overnight or for at least 4 hours, turning the meat occasionally.

Preheat a grill to very high. Remove the meat from the marinade and pat dry. Season with salt. Carefully place the meat on the grill and seal on both sides. Lower the heat and continue to grill until the desired degree of pinkness, turning once. Allow at least 8 minutes per side.

Rognoncini con Carciofi e Timo
Kidneys with Artichoke Hearts and Thyme

Serves 6

3 whole calf's kidneys in their fat

6 globe artichokes, prepared and cut into sixths (see page 148)

6 tablespoons olive oil

3 garlic cloves, peeled and sliced

2 heaped teaspoons fresh thyme leaves

2 dried chillies, crumbled

sea salt and freshly ground black pepper

120 ml (4 fl oz) white wine

lemon juice

1 tablespoon chopped flat-leaf parsley

Remove the fat and peel off the thin membrane surrounding the kidneys. With a short sharp knife, halve the kidneys and remove the central core. Cut the kidneys into their natural segments. While doing this, more fat and gristle may become apparent, which should be trimmed. The pieces should be of similar size.

Heat half the oil in a large frying pan and fry the artichoke pieces until they start to brown. Add the garlic, thyme and chilli, and fry until the garlic starts to colour. Add about 120 ml (4 fl oz) water and some salt and cook until the water has evaporated and the artichokes are tender. Put to one side and wipe the pan clean.

Heat the remaining oil in the pan over a high heat until it begins to smoke. Add the kidneys and seal on each side. Cook for 2 minutes if you like your kidneys pink, or longer if you like them more well done. Finally, add the wine, reduce quickly, then return the artichokes to the pan and heat through. Season to taste, then add the lemon juice and parsley.

Fegato di Vitello con Cavolo Nero
Pan-Fried Calf's Liver with Cavolo Nero

Serves 2

2 thick slices calf's liver

sea salt and freshly ground black pepper

1 tablespoon extra virgin olive oil

50 ml (2 fl oz) balsamic vinegar

50 ml (2 fl oz) crème fraîche

To serve

Braised Cavolo Nero (see page 184)

Cook the cavolo nero, and keep warm.

Season the liver on both sides with salt and pepper. Brush a large frying pan with olive oil and, when very hot, fry the liver for 1 minute on each side. Add the balsamic vinegar and turn the liver so that it absorbs the vinegar which will reduce almost immediately. Add the crème fraîche and let it melt into the vinegar. Remove and serve on top of the cavolo nero, pouring over some of the sauce made in the pan.

Poached Brains

Serves 6

3 calf's brains

4 tablespoons white wine vinegar

Soak the brains in cold water for at least an hour. Remove the membranes and blood vessels from the inner contours of the brains: this is most easily done under gently running cold water. It is easier to clean the brains if they are divided in half at the cortex.

Heat a saucepan of water with the vinegar; when boiling, lower the heat and gently add the brains, and simmer for 10 minutes. Leave to cool in the water.

The brains are now ready for use in the opposite recipe.

Poached Sweetbreads

Serves 6

2 whole calf's sweetbreads

juice of 1 lemon

Wash and soak the sweetbreads in cold water for an hour. Put in a saucepan and cover with cold water and the lemon juice. Bring to the boil and simmer gently, for 15-20 minutes, depending on size. Leave to cool in the water.

When cool enough to handle, drain, peel off the membrane and gristle, keeping the sweetbreads in one piece if possible.

The sweetbreads are now ready for use in the recipe opposite.

Cervelle e Animelle in Padella
Pan-Fried Calf's Brains and Sweetbreads

Serves 6

3 poached calf's brains

2 whole poached calf's sweetbreads (see opposite)

100 g (4 oz) plain flour

sea salt and freshly ground black pepper

2 tablespoons olive oil

50 g (2 oz) unsalted butter

24 sage leaves

3 tablespoons salted capers, prepared (see page 306)

juice of 2 lemons

Cut each half brain in half again. Slice the sweetbreads lengthways into six even slices or, alternatively, slice diagonally into discs. Dust with a scant amount of seasoned flour.

Heat the oil and half the butter in a large frying pan. When hot, add the brains and sweetbreads and fry until light brown on one side. Sprinkle the sage leaves and capers over the brains and sweetbreads and turn. Add the remaining butter and continue to fry to brown the second side. Lower the heat, and season. Squeeze in the lemon juice and serve.

Salsicce Piccanti
Spiced Italian Sausages

Serves 6

Quick Sweet Tomato Sauce (see page 273)

12 Italian spicy pork sausages, ideally luganega

6 bay leaves

10 black peppercorns

olive oil

Wet Polenta (see page 120)

Parmesan, freshly grated

While the sauce is simmering, put the sausages, bay leaves and peppercorns in a frying pan. Pour in enough water to barely cover the sausages, and cook over a medium heat until the water has evaporated, turning the sausages several times. This can take about an hour. Pour away the pork fat from the sausages and add 1 tablespoon olive oil. Lower the heat and gently fry the sausages for a few minutes on either side.

Pour the tomato sauce over the sausages and heat through.

Put the polenta on a large, warm plate. Make a hollow in the centre with the back of a spoon and fill with the tomato sauce and sausages. Serve with Parmesan.

Salsicce River Cafe
Fresh Spiced Sausages

Makes about 12 sausages

400 g (14 oz) fresh pork belly or shoulder

200 g (7 oz) breast of veal

150 g (5 oz) prosciutto crudo ends

150 g (5 oz) pancetta or coppa ends

20 g (3/4 oz) fennel seeds

25 g (1 oz) black peppercorns

sea salt

sausage skins, soaked in cold water

Put all the meats through a mincer, then mixed together in a bowl. You can use a food processor, but it is essential that th eblade has been sharpened and only pulse-chop very small quantities of each meat at a time.

Grind the fennel seeds and about half of the peppercorns in a mortar. Add to the meat mixture, along with some salt and the remaining peppercorns. Mix well, then stuff into the skins.

Cook as in the previous recipe or grill over a low heat.

Bollito Misto

This is the classic dish for New Year's Eve in northern Italy. The lentils symbolise wealth, the meat health, and the mostarda, good spirits for the year to come.

Serves 8-10

1 small ox tongue, about 1.2 – 1.5 kg (2.1/2-3.1/2 lb) in weight

1 large boiling fowl or capon, about 2.25 – 2.75 kg (5-6 lb) in weight

2 pre-cooked cotechino sausages, or zampone di Modena

20 carrots, scrubbed

3 celery hearts, each divided lengthways into quarters

sea salt and freshly ground black pepper

For the stock

1 bunch parsley stalks (use the leaves for the accompanying Salsa Verde, see page 270)

1 head garlic, cut in half

4 carrots, scrubbed

4 bay leaves

2 red onions, peeled

2 tablespoons black peppercorns

outside celery sticks, from the hearts

Soak the tongue in cold water, preferably for 24 hours, but at least 4-5 hours. Drain and place in a large saucepan. Cover with water and add half the stock ingredients. Simmer for 3 hours, skimming off any scum as it comes to the surface, until the tongue is soft and a fork or skewer can be easily inserted. Remove the tongue from the stock and place on a board. Peel off the skin – it should come away easily. Return the skinned tongue to the saucepan and cook for a further 30 minutes.

After the tongue has been cooking for 2 hours, put the boiling fowl in another large saucepan and cover with water. Add the remaining stock ingredients and very gently simmer for 1.3/4-2.1/2 hours, depending on size.

Cook the sausages according to the instructions on the packet. Zampone are larger and will take 40 minutes to cook. Cotechino will be ready in 20 minutes.

Add the carrots and celery hearts to the chicken 20 minutes before serving. Season with a little salt.

Turn off the heat under the three pans and keep the meats in their various stocks. Taste the chicken stock and add more salt if necessary.

To serve, cut the tongue into 5 mm (1/4 in) thick slices; the chicken (some white and some brown meat) into similar slices; and the sausages into 8 mm (1/3 in) slices. Arrange on a large warm serving plate and pour over some of the strained chicken stock. Arrange the carrot and celery around the meats.

Serve with Salsa Verde, mostarda di Cremona and lentils (see pages 270, 309 and 171).

Variation Veal or beef silverside (1.2 – 1.5 kg/2.1/2-3.1/2 lb) can be cooked in the same way and for the same time as the tongue, but you should add 3-4 plum tomatoes either tinned or fresh and 50 g (2 oz) dried porcini to the stock ingredients.

Poult
and C

ry
Game
7

In Italy game does not have the aristocratic connotations it has in Britain. In season, even the simplest trattoria will have some form of game on the menu, especially in Tuscany and Umbria.

The strong and definite flavours of game birds allow us to handle them in an Italian way. Instead of the standard bacon fat used in Britain, we wrap the birds in pancetta or prosciutto, each of which has its own distinct flavour. The game season coincides with the harvesting of maize for polenta, of chestnuts, and the arrival of the new olive oil – ingredients we love most with game. The bird cavities can be stuffed with the livers, with cotechino sausage, chestnuts, thyme, sage or mostarda di cremona. If we use bread with game, it will not be the classic bread sauce, but rather a slice of bruschetta rubbed with garlic and strong olive oil, or spread with the birds' livers cooked in red wine with sage and thyme.

Unlike game, chicken has no season. Rather than make sauces for chicken, we prefer to stuff them under the skin, allowing the flavour – as in marinating – to permeate the meat. When cooked some of the stuffing will ooze out and combine to form a natural sauce.

Pollo alla Griglia
Marinated Grilled Chicken

Serves 2

1 x 1.1 kg (2.1/2 lb) free-range or corn-fed chicken

juice of 1 lemon

25 g (1 oz) very coarsely ground black pepper

sea salt and black pepper

olive oil (optional)

To bone a chicken: place the chicken, breast side up, on a board. With a sharp boning knife, cut along the breast bone, then guide the knife, cutting between breast and carcass on one side, down to the leg joint. You have to cut the wishbone in half to divide the breast at its centre. Crack the leg bone at the joint away from the carcass so that it lies flat on the board. With the knife, carefully cut around the joint, separating the whole of one side from its carcass. Repeat this with the other side.

Snip the wing tips from the wings, leaving the bone in the short part of the wing. To remove the bones from the legs, flatten out your chicken half skin side down. Using the leg bones as a guide, cut as close to them on either side as possible, and then insert the tip of the knife and prise up one bone, cutting as you do so. It is always difficult near the joint between thigh and drumstick, but you must try not to cut the skin which ultimately will hold your stuffing (see next two recipes). Trim any flabby bits of skin and cut away any pieces of fat.

In a deep dish large enough to contain the two pieces, place some of the lemon juice, some black pepper and the pieces of chicken, skin side down. Sprinkle with pepper and more lemon juice. Cover with cling film and leave to marinate for anything from 2 to 24 hours.

Preheat a grill to very hot.

Place the chicken pieces skin side up on the hottest part of the grill. Sprinkle with salt and seal for a minute, then turn over and place on a cooler part of the grill or lower the heat. Salt the other side and continue to grill, turning from time to time, until the chicken is cooked.

Pollo Spago

This recipe is adapted from one served at Wolfgang Puck's famous restaurant Spago in Los Angeles.

Serves 2

1 x 1.1 kg (2.1/2 lb) free-range or corn-fed chicken, boned (see page 244)

8 garlic cloves, peeled

100 g (4 oz) flat-leaf parsley, chopped

sea salt and freshly ground black pepper

3 tablespoons olive oil

Wipe the chicken halves thoroughly. Loosen the side from the meat making two pockets, one at the breast end and one at the leg end.

Place the garlic cloves in a small saucepan of cold water and bring to the boil. Cook for 2 minutes, then drain and chop the cloves. Mix the cooked chopped garlic and parsley together, and use half the mixture to stuff in the pockets. Season the chicken with salt and pepper. Grill the chicken halves for about 20 minutes at medium-high heat, turning frequently, until they are crisp and golden and cooked through.

Heat the olive oil in a small saucepan, add the remaining garlic and parsley mixture and cook gently. Season with salt and pepper. Spoon over the chicken and serve.

Pollo Ripieno con Mascarpone
Pan-Fried Chicken with Mascarpone

Serves 2

1 x 1.2-1.5 kg (2.1/2 – 3 lb) free-range or corn-fed chicken, boned (see page 244)

2 tablespoons very finely chopped fresh rosemary leaves

4 tablespoons mascarpone cheese

sea salt and freshly ground black pepper

1 tablespoon olive oil

juice of 1.1/2 lemons

Preheat the oven to 230°C/450°F/Gas 8.

Prepare the chicken as in the previous recipe, making pockets for the stuffing.

Mix the rosemary with the mascarpone, season with salt and pepper, and place a large tablespoonful of this mixture in each pocket in the chicken. Season the chicken with salt and pepper.

Heat the oil in a large ovenproof frying pan. Brown the chicken pieces quickly on both sides, put into the preheated oven and roast for about 15 minutes. Test for doneness by pulling a leg away from the body, if the juices run pink, cook a little longer. Remove the pan from the oven and over a medium heat, add the lemon juice. It will immediately combine with the mascarpone and chicken juices. Turn the chicken to coat it with the sauce and serve.

Pernice con Prosciutto
Partridge Wrapped in Prosciutto

We cook grouse and woodcock in the same manner.

Serves 6

6 partridges, plucked and cleaned

sea salt and freshly ground black pepper

6 fresh thyme sprigs

6 large slices prosciutto

100 g (4 oz) dried porcini mushrooms, reconstituted (see page 312)

olive oil

2 garlic cloves, peeled and chopped

300 ml (10 fl oz) red wine

300 g (10 oz) freshly cooked Wet Polenta (see page 120)

150 g (5 oz) butter

150 g (5 oz) Parmesan, freshly grated

Season the partridges inside and out, and put the thyme sprigs in the cavities. Place the prosciutto slices over the breast and legs of the birds, and tie on with string.

Drain the soaked porcini, straining and reserving the liquid. Rinse the porcini well under cold running water.

Heat 2 tablespoons olive oil in a small frying pan and gently cook the garlic until light brown, along with any remaining thyme leaves and the porcini. Fry for a further minute, then add about 300 ml (10 fl oz) of the strained porcini liquid. Continue to simmer gently, adding more liquid if necessary, until the mushrooms are tender, and there are no juices left, about 15 minutes.

Preheat the oven to 230-240°C/450-475°F/Gas 8-9.

In a large roasting pan, heat 2 further tablespoons of oil and brown the birds on each side on top of the stove. Roast in the very hot oven for 10 minutes, then turn the birds over. Add the mushrooms and half the wine. Return to the oven for a further 5-10 minutes, depending on how rare you like your birds.

Stir 50 g (2 oz) of the butter and 75 g (3 oz) of the Parmesan into the polenta.

To serve, spoon the polenta on to warm plates then place a partridge on top with some of the porcini. Deglaze the pan quickly with the remaining wine and butter. Season, then pour over the bird and polenta. Sprinkle with the remaining Parmesan.

Piccione Ripieno con Cotechino
Pan-roasted Pigeon Stuffed with Cotechino

Serves 6

6 Bresse pigeons, plucked and cleaned

25 ml (1 fl oz) olive oil

sea salt and freshly ground black pepper

250 ml (8 fl oz) red wine and/or Chicken or Veal Stock (see page 54)

For the stuffing

2 small red onions, peeled and chopped

4 celery stalks, chopped

2 tablespoons olive oil

1 cotechino sausage

20 sage leaves, shredded

250 ml (8 fl oz) red wine

Preheat the oven to 230°C/450°F/Gas 8.

Make the stuffing. Soften the onion and celery in the oil for 10 minutes over a low heat. Remove the skin of the cotechino and crumble the meat with your hands. Add the cotechino and sage to the onion and celery and fry for 10 minutes. Pour off the fat from the pan, add the red wine and boil to reduce by at least half. Season with pepper and allow to cool before stuffing into the birds.

Heat 25 ml (1 fl oz) oil in a roasting pan over a medium to high heat, and brown each bird all over. Season with salt and pepper, place in the top of the preheated oven and roast for 20 minutes.

Remove the pan from the oven, and take out the pigeon. Keep warm. Pour any excess oil out of the pan, then place over a medium heat and add the red wine and/or stock. Over a high heat reduce the liquid in the pan by half, then season with salt and pepper. Pour over the pigeon.

Tetraone Cucinato nella Pancetta
Roast Grouse with Pancetta

Per person

  1 grouse, plucked and cleaned

  1 chicken liver, finely chopped

  5 thin slices pancetta

  2 large sprigs fresh thyme

  1 garlic clove, peeled and chopped

  25 g (1 oz) butter

  250 ml (8 fl oz) sweet red wine (such as Aleatico di Puglia or Recioto della Valpolicella)

  sea salt and freshly ground black pepper

  1 tablespoon olive oil

To make the stuffing, mix the liver with two of the pancetta slices cut into matchsticks, the leaves of one of the sprigs of thyme and the chopped garlic, then brown in the butter in a small pan. This will only take a few minutes. When a good colour, add 175 ml (6 fl oz) of the wine, boil to reduce a little, season and cool.

Spoon this stuffing into the cavity of the bird. Place the remaining thyme sprig on the breast of the bird, cover with the remaining pancetta slices, and tie on with string, crossing the string to tie the legs together so that the stuffing does not fall out.

Preheat the oven to 230°C/450°F/Gas 8.

Brush a suitably sized roasting pan with the olive oil, heat, and seal the grouse well on the back, legs and each breast. This is especially important if the grouse is well hung and quite high. Place in the oven and roast for 20-30 minutes, depending on size and how rare you like grouse. We serve them slightly pink. The easiest way to test for doneness is to pull the leg away from the body at the thigh. If still blue, cook for a little longer. Grouse vary in roasting time because they differ so much in size.

Leave the bird to rest for 2-3 minutes, then remove from the pan and untie the string. Heat the roasting pan, add the remaining wine and reduce by half. Return the bird to the pan and turn to coat it in the juices.

Stuffing Variations

Mostarda di Cremona Take four pieces of fruit from a small jar of mostarda di Cremona and chop. Mince and fry about 50 g (2 oz) fresh pork belly in 2 tablespoons in olive oil for a few seconds then add 1 chopped garlic clove and 1 small sprig of thyme. Chop 25 g (1 oz) coppa di Parma into ribbons and add to the pan, along with the mostarda fruit. Season and, when cool, place 1 heaped tablespoon inside each bird.

Dolcetta Use 1 large tablespoon dolcetta jam per bird, plus a slice of pancetta.

Quince cheese (see page 294) can be used in the same way. Use 1 tablespoon per bird along with a slice of pancetta and a sprig of thyme.

Brasato di Fagiano con Cavolo
Braised Pheasant with Cabbage

Serves 4

2 x 675 g – 1.1 kg (1.1/2 – 2.1/2 lb) young pheasants

1 small Savoy cabbage, shredded and blanched

2 tablespoons olive oil

100 g (4 oz) pancetta, cut into matchsticks

2 garlic cloves, peeled and thinly sliced

175 ml (6 fl oz) red wine

300 ml (10 fl oz) Chicken Stock (see page 54)

Preheat the oven to 230°C/450°F/Gas 8.

Heat the oil in a saucepan just large enough to hold the pheasants. Over a medium-high heat brown the pheasants well all over, one at a time. Remove from the saucepan and place in a roasting pan. Roast in the preheated oven for 20 minutes, then let the birds relax for 5 minutes.

Add the pancetta to the saucepan and fry until brown. Add the sliced garlic and cook for a minute. Pour in the wine and boil to reduce. Now add the cabbage and sufficient stock to combine.

With a large knife cut the birds in half through the breast bone. Gently turn the pheasant halves in the pancetta and cabbage mixture. Cover with a tight-fitting lid. Cook very gently together over a low heat for 15 minutes.

Fagiano Arrosto con Cotogne
Roast Pheasant with Quince

Serves 6

3 x 675 g – 1.1 kg (1.1/2 – 2.1/2 lb) young pheasants

6 tablespoons Quince Cheese (see page 294)

3 large handfuls fresh thyme

9 slices coppa di Parma

sea salt and freshly ground black pepper

2 tablespoons olive oil

1/2 bottle Chianti Classico

Braised Cavolo Nero (see page 184)

Preheat the oven to 220°C/425°F/Gas 7.

Place 2 tablespoons of the cheese, a third of the thyme and 1 slice of coppa inside each pheasant. Place another 2 slices of coppa over each breast, and tie on with string. Season with salt and pepper.

Heat the oil in an ovenproof dish large enough to hold the birds, and quickly brown on all sides. Pour in half of the red wine, and let it bubble for a minute or two to reduce slightly. Place the dish in the preheated oven, the birds breast-side up, and roast for 25-35 minutes. To test for doneness, pull away a leg from the body. If the meat is pink and you like your bird rare it is ready.

Remove from the oven. Add the remainder of the wine, stir into the roasting juices and boil to reduce over a high heat.

To serve, cut each pheasant in two down the breastbone. Place each half on a warm plate covered with cabbage, and pour over the roasting juices.

Fagiano in Josephine Dore
Pheasant with Josephine Dore

Serves 6

3 x 6.75 g – 1.1 kg (1.1/2 – 2.1/2 lb) pheasants

6 slices prosciutto or pancetta affumicata

120 ml (4 fl oz) olive oil

100 g (4 oz) butter

6 garlic cloves, peeled

6 sprigs rosemary

10 sage leaves

1 bottle Josephine Dore (see glossary), or dry white port

350 ml (12 fl oz) Chicken Stock (see page 54)

250 ml (8 fl oz) double cream

sea salt and freshly ground black pepper

Place the prosciutto slices over the pheasant breasts, and tie on with string.

Heat the oil and butter in a heavy-bottomed saucepan and brown the pheasants on all sides. Add the garlic and herbs, then cook, turning the birds frequently over a medium heat, for about 40 minutes adding the wine and stock in stages: you do not want to boil the birds but braise them in the liquid, which should just cover the bottom of the pan.

Remove the birds and keep warm. If there is a lot of juice, reduce over a high heat, then add the cream. Let simmer and thicken, then season with salt and pepper. Pour the juices over the pheasants.

Piccione Ripieno di Castagne
Pan-roasted Bresse Pigeon with Chestnuts

Serves 6

6 Bresse pigeons (not wild pigeons)

6 slices prosciutto

1 tablespoon olive oil

150 ml (5 fl oz) Dolcetta wine from Piedmont

For the stuffing

450 g (1 lb) fresh chestnuts or 250 g (9 oz) vacuum-packed peeled chestnuts

1 tablespoon olive oil

1 red onion, peeled and finely chopped

2 garlic cloves, peeled and chopped

175 g (6 oz) fresh belly of pork, minced

2 tablespoons fresh thyme leaves

100 g (4 oz) pancetta affumicata, chopped

150 ml (5 fl oz) Dolcetta wine

1 teaspoon crushed juniper berries

1/4 nutmeg, grated

sea salt and freshly ground black pepper

Make the stuffing. To prepare the fresh chestnuts, make a cut in the skin on the flat side. Grill on both sides, then place immediately into a bowl lined with a dampened hot cloth. Cover with the cloth and leave until cool enough to handle. The skins should come off very easily. Break the chestnuts into small pieces.

Heat the oil in a pan and fry the onion until soft, about 10 minutes. Add the garlic, fresh pork and thyme, and cook, stirring, until the pork is brown. Add the pancetta, the wine, juniper and nutmeg and cook together for a further 5 minutes. Season with salt and pepper. Remove from the heat.

Preheat the oven to 230°C/450°F/Gas 8.

Add the chestnut pieces to the cool stuffing and then stuff each bird. Cover the pigeon breasts with the slices of prosciutto and tie on with string. Brush a suitable roasting pan with the oil and brown the birds all over. Roast them in the preheated oven for 20 minutes. Test by pulling a leg away: if still too pink, cook for a little longer.

Remove the birds from the pan and keep warm. Deglaze the juices in the pan with the wine, and pour over the birds. Serve with Wet Polenta, Smashed Celeriac or Braised Cavolo Nero (see pages 120, 175 and 184).

Anatra Arrosto al Vino Rosso
Roast Duck with Sweet Red Wine

Buy small Gressingham ducks and allow half a duck per person. The ducks are blanched before roasting to release the excess fat.

Serves 6

3 ducks, with their livers

3 handfuls fresh rosemary leaves, very finely chopped

3 handfuls fresh sage leaves, very finely chopped

sea salt and freshly ground black pepper

1 bottle sweet red wine (such as Aleatico di Puglia)

2 tablespoons olive oil

2 garlic cloves, peeled and chopped

Fill a saucepan large enough to hold all the ducks with water and bring to the boil. Lower the heat to a simmer and immerse the ducks. Leave small ducks in for 5 minutes; larger, fattier ones for 7-8 minutes. Remove the ducks and hang over a dish to collect the liquid fat that will drip out. Allow to drip for 30 minutes, longer if possible. Using a hairdryer, blow hot air over the skin surface to assist the release of the fat.

Mix together the rosemary and sage with a generous amount of salt.

Roughly chop the duck livers, then place in a blender with 250 ml (8 fl oz) of the wine, 2 tablespoons of the herb and salt mixture, the olive oil and garlic. Blend until you have a thick liquid.

Pour a third of the liver and herb mixture into the tail cavity of each duck, swirling it around to coat the interior. Push the tail into the cavity to close it. Then rub every part of the skin with the remaining herb and salt mixture; this should adhere well as the ducks will be very greasy.

Preheat the oven to 220°C/430°F/Gas 7. Place the ducks on wire racks inside roasting trays, breast side up, and roast for 30 minutes – the skin should quickly begin to brown. Then lower the oven temperature to 190°C/375°F/Gas 5. Turn the ducks over and continue to roast for about an hour. The ducks are cooked when the flesh comes away from the bone and the skin is crisp.

Pour off the duck fat from the trays, but keep the juices if any – most of the juice will be inside the ducks, held in by the tail.

Pour the juices into the tray, add the remaining wine and boil to reduce to a syrup. Season well. Serve this as a sauce with the duck.

Sau

ces

8

Of all our recipes, the sauces we make at the River Cafe are the most basic and yet most difficult to get right. As there are so few ingredients involved in most of the sauces, and rarely any cooking, the quality of ingredients is essential. The olive oil *must* be the best extra virgin, the salt *must* be Maldon sea salt, the parsley *must* be flat leaf, the anchovies *must* be salted.

In traditional Italian cooking there are, in fact, few sauces for meat or fish as most often they will be served with olive oil and a generous piece of lemon. But we love fresh chopped red chilli sauce with squid, roasted red chillis in olive oil on grilled lamb or steak, salmoriglio with monkfish or scallops. And we also love chillis on monkfish, anchovy and rosemary sauce on lamb and almost any of the sauces in this chapter on grilled polenta or bruschetta.

Salsa verde, salsa rossa and salmoriglio are a few of the basic and well known sauces found in Italy, and are intrinsic to many regional classic dishes. We have adapted these recipes and their uses towards our style of cooking.

There are no rules or strict measures. It is essential to keep tasting as the proportions you use will depend on the strength of the ingredients. We suggest you try sauces with various foods, remembering that the objective is to enhance rather than mask the flavour, and that if the flavour of the sauce is intense to use it sparingly.

Salsa Calda d'Acciughe e Rosmarino
Hot Anchovy Sauce

12 salted anchovy fillets, prepared

    (see page 304)

2 teaspoons finely chopped rosemary

freshly ground black pepper

2 teaspoons lemon juice

100 g (4 oz) unsalted butter

Place the anchovies, rosemary and a pinch of pepper in a mortar and pound to a smooth paste. Add the lemon juice, and stir well.

Gently melt the butter in a small saucepan, and add the anchovy paste. Stir constantly until warm but do not allow to boil.

Salsa Fredda d'Acciughe e Rosmarino
Anchovy and Rosemary Sauce

2 tablespoons finely chopped rosemary

12 salted anchovy fillets, prepared

    (see page304)

juice of 2 lemons

150 ml (5 fl oz) extra virgin olive oil

Crush the rosemary in a mortar, add the anchovies and pound to a paste. Slowly add the lemon juice, stirring to blend. Finally add the olive oil a drop at a time. When about half has been added, pour in the remainder in a thin, steady stream, stirring continuously.

Alternatively, you can use a food processor although this method produces a thicker sauce. Put the rosemary in and chop very finely, then add the anchovy and chop to a thick, fine paste. Pour the oil in slowly. Finally, add the lemon juice.

Salsa di Peperoncini Scottati
Grilled Chilli Sauce

6 medium fresh red chillies

6 tablespoons olive oil

sea salt

2 tablespoons lemon juice

Grill the chillies until the skin is black and blistered. Whilst still hot seal in a small plastic bag or put in a bowl and cover with cling film and allow to cool.

Pull the skins from the chillies, cut in half from top to bottom and remove the seeds. Put in a bowl, cover with oil, and season with a little salt and the lemon juice.

Salsa di Peperoncini Rossi
Fresh Red Chilli Sauce

6 red chillies, seeded and finely
   chopped

25 g (1 oz) flat-leaf parsley, chopped

1 garlic clove, peeled and finely
   chopped

salt and freshly ground black pepper

120 ml (4 fl oz) extra virgin olive oil

Combine the chillies, parsley and garlic. Season with salt and pepper, and pour the oil over the top.

Salsa di Mascarpone e Gorgonzola
Gorgonzola and Mascarpone Sauce

50 g (2 oz) butter

2 tablespoons finely chopped marjoram, oregano or basil leaves

250 g (9 oz) mascarpone cheese

150 g (5 oz) Gorgonzola cheese

sea salt and freshly ground black pepper

Gently melt the butter in a saucepan – do not let it brown – and add the herbs. Add the mascarpone and Gorgonzola and warm through very gently until melted. Season with salt and pepper.

Note 400 g (14 oz) Torta di Dolcelatte or Torta di Gorgonzola can be substituted for the mascarpone and Gorgonzola.

Salsa di Erbe
Fresh Herb Sauce

1/2 stale ciabatta or similar loaf

1 tablespoon red wine vinegar

2 garlic cloves, peeled and crushed

2 tablespoons salted capers, chopped

4 salted anchovies, chopped

1 fresh red chilli, seeded and chopped

sea salt and freshly ground black pepper

8 tablespoons mixed fresh herbs (mint, basil, oregano, marjoram, parsley)

75 ml (2.1/2 fl oz) extra virgin olive oil

Soak the bread in the red wine vinegar and 1/2 cup water for 10 minutes. Remove and squeeze out the liquid, and put the bread in a large bowl.

Add the crushed garlic, capers and chopped anchovies, and incorporate into the bread. Add the chilli and season.

Chop a generous amount of each herb and mix into the bread. Slowly pour in the olive oil in a steady stream until the sauce has a rough, thick, bready texture.

Bagnet
Anchovy Sauce

1/4 ciabatta loaf

6 salted anchovy fillets, prepared

    (see page 304) and finely chopped

3 tablespoons finely chopped

    flat-leaf parsley

1 tablespoon salted capers, prepared (see

    page 306) and finely chopped

1 garlic clove, peeled and crushed

2 hard-boiled egg yolks

1 tablespoon white wine vinegar

2 tablespoons extra virgin olive oil

1/4 teaspoon freshly ground

    black pepper

Soak the bread in 1/2 cup water, then squeeze out the liquid. Mix the bread with the anchovies, parsley, capers, garlic and egg yolks, using a fork. Add the vinegar, oil and pepper.

Salmoriglio
Oregano Sauce

A salmoriglio is a fresh herb sauce, in which the flavour of the herb is brought out by crushing it with sea salt. It is very intense, so should be used sparingly.

4 level tablespoons fresh oregano

1 teaspoon sea salt

2 tablespoons lemon juice

8 tablespoons extra virgin olive oil

freshly ground black pepper

In a pestle and mortar pound the herb leaves with the salt until completely crushed. Add the lemon juice. Pour the oil slowly into the mixture. Add a little pepper.

Variation Marjoram, thyme or lemon thyme can be substituted for oregano.

Salsa Rossa
Red Sauce

2 red peppers, grilled (see page 140)

4 ripe fresh tomatoes, skinned, or 1 x 250 g

    (8 oz) tin plum tomatoes, drained of

    their juices

2 tablespoons olive oil

1 garlic clove, peeled and finely

    chopped

1 fresh red chilli, seeded and finely

    chopped

1 tablespoon fresh marjoram leaves

sea salt and freshly ground

    black pepper

2 small dried chillies, crumbled

Peel and seed the peppers, then chop the flesh finely.

Heat the olive oil in a saucepan and gently fry the garlic until it starts to colour. Add the chilli and whole marjoram leaves and tomatoes and cook for 30 minutes or until the tomatoes are reduced. Add the peppers and cook for a further 10 minutes. Season with salt and pepper and dried chilli.

Salsa Verde
Green Sauce

1 large bunch flat-leaf parsley

1 bunch fresh basil

a handful of fresh mint leaves

3 garlic cloves, peeled

100 g (4 oz) salted capers, prepared

    (see page 306)

100 g (4 oz) salted anchovies, prepared

    (see page 304)

2 tablespoons red wine vinegar

5 tablespoons extra virgin olive oil

1 tablespoon Dijon mustard

sea salt

freshly ground black pepper

If using a food processor, pulse-chop the parsley, basil, mint, garlic, capers and anchovies until roughly blended. Transfer to a large bowl and add the vinegar. Slowly pour in the olive oil, stirring constantly, and finally add the mustard. Check for seasoning.

This sauce may also be prepared by hand, on a board, preferably using a mezzaluna.

Salsa Pasta d'Olive
Olive Sauce

225 g (8 oz) calamata or other strong

   black olives

1 fresh red chilli, seeded and finely

   chopped

1 garlic clove, peeled and crushed

120 ml (4 fl oz) extra virgin olive oil

sea salt

freshly ground black pepper

Stone the olives and roughly chop, ideally with a mezzaluna. Place in a bowl and add the chilli and garlic, cover with olive oil, and season if necessary.

This sauce may also be made in a food processor. Briefly pulse-chop the olives, then add the chilli and garlic, and again briefly pulse-chop. Avoid over-processing and ending up with a paste.

Salsa di Dragoncello
Tarragon Sauce

1/2 ciabatta loaf

65 ml (2.1/2 fl oz) red wine vinegar

the yolks of 2 hard-boiled eggs

100 g (4 oz) fresh tarragon, stalks removed,

   chopped

10 salted anchovy fillets, prepared (see

   page 304), chopped

50 g (2 oz) salted capers, prepared (see

   page 306), chopped

120-175 ml (4-6 fl oz) extra virgin olive oil

Tear the bread into small pieces, and soak in the vinegar for 20 minutes. Remove, squeeze dry, and chop, ideally with a mezzaluna.

Mash the egg yolks with a fork.

Very gently combine the bread, tarragon, anchovies, capers and egg in a bowl. Stir in the oil.

Aioli di Mandorle
Almond Aioli

the crust of 1 ciabatta loaf, cut into

large pieces

4 garlic cloves, peeled

100 g (4 oz) whole blanched

almonds, roasted

2 egg yolks

250 ml (8 fl oz) olive oil

juice of 2-3 lemons

sea salt and freshly ground

black pepper

Soak the crusts in cold water until soft. Squeeze dry.

Pound the garlic and almonds together in a mortar with the pestle until a paste, then add the crusts and pound well to mix thoroughly. Add and mix in the egg yolks.

Pour in the olive oil little by little, stirring with the pestle all the time. When it becomes too thick to stir, thin with a little lemon juice. Continue to add the olive oil. Add more lemon juice to taste and then season. Aioli should have a rough, thick texture.

Maionese
Mayonnaise

2 egg yolks

500 ml (17 fl oz) extra virgin olive oil

lemon juice

sea salt and freshly ground black pepper

Put the egg yolks in the mortar. Break them with the pestle and stir, blending them together. Add the oil, drip by drip, stirring all the time. When you have added half the oil, and the mixture is very thick and sticky, thin with a little lemon juice. When you have a perfect emulsion, add the oil in a slow flow rather than in drips.

You may not use all the oil, as egg yolks vary in size, and you may actually like a thicker consistency if using with vegetables or fish. If so add more lemon juice, salt and pepper to taste.

Variation For a basil mayonnaise, pound 3 large handfuls of basil in a pestle and mortar with a little salt. Add the egg yolks and blend together. Then add the olive oil as described above.

Sugo di Pomodoro Veloce
Quick Sweet Tomato Sauce

This sauce requires a large pan so the surface remains very hot. It is particularly good served with grilled or deep-fried salt cod, or a dried pasta such as penne.

2 x 800 g (1.3/4 lb) tins plum tomatoes,

    drained of their juices

3 tablespoons olive oil

3 garlic cloves, peeled and cut into slivers

sea salt and freshly ground black pepper

a handful of fresh basil or oregano leaves

Heat 1-2 tablespoons of the oil in a pan, and fry the garlic until it is soft but not brown. Add the tomatoes, some salt and pepper and cook fiercely, stirring constantly to prevent the tomatoes from sticking as they break up. As they cook, the tomatoes will release their juices. When this liquid has evaporated, add the remaining olive oil, the basil or oregano, and more seasoning if necessary. Serve hot.

Sugo di Pomodoro a Fuoco Lento
Slow-Cooked Tomato Sauce

2 x 800 g (1.3/4 lb) tins plum tomatoes,

    drained of their juices

3 tablespoons olive oil

4 medium red onions, peeled and sliced as

    thinly as possible into rounds

2 garlic cloves, peeled and cut into slivers

In a large saucepan or frying pan, heat the oil, then add the onions. Reduce the heat and cook the onions until they are very soft. The onions must disappear into the tomato sauce. This will take at least 40 minutes. Some 5 minutes before the end of cooking, add the garlic.

Now add the tomatoes and stir to break them up. Season with salt and pepper and cook slowly, stirring occasionally, for at least 1.1/2 hours. The oil should come to the surface and the sauce will be dark red and extremely thick, with no juice at all.

Dess

serts

9

Meals in Italy usually end with a strong espresso. Cakes and pastries are more often eaten at breakfast than as a dessert, and ice creams in the street.

Not all the desserts in this chapter are Italian but they are consistent with the food we cook at the River Cafe – strong in flavour and uncomplicated. Our lemon tart has more lemon than eggs, the chocolate cakes have no flour and depend on the best and most bitter chocolate; ripe peaches are simply grilled and then marinated in Amaretto. Our ice creams are intense with a larger than usual proportion of egg yolks to milk and cream, but this richness is offset by making them less sweet.

Some of our recipes, such as Zabaglione ice cream, have Italian origins but have been adapted to British ingredients. This ice cream was conceived by Dada Rogers, an Italian living in wartime London, who found the combination of dark rum and Bristol Cream sherry a good substitute for the traditional but unobtainable Marsala. Others, such as Polenta almond and lemon cake originate elsewhere but have been made more italian by the use of ingredients.

There is also a seasonal quality to our desserts. In summer we make sorbets, raspberry, strawberry, or black currant with only lemon and sugar; in winter we make ice creams with the bitter flavour of burned caramel, dark chocolate, or vanilla. In summer our almond tarts are covered with uncooked fruit, in winter pears are cooked under the almond filling, resulting in a tart with a denser texture.

The most popular dessert at the River Cafe, and one that transcends both seasons and cultures, is Chocolate Nemesis.

Pere al Forno con Marsala e Cannella
Pears Baked with Marsala and Cinnamon

Serves 6

6 ripe Comice pears

50 g (2 oz) unsalted butter, at room temperature

100 g (4 oz) soft dark brown sugar

175 ml (6 fl oz) Marsala

50 ml (2 fl oz) white wine

2 cinnamon sticks, roughly broken

crème fraîche

Preheat the oven to 180°C/350°F/Gas 4.

Cut a small slice from the rounded end of each pear so that it will stand up, then remove the core. Spread a little butter over the skin of each pear and stand them in an ovenproof dish. Dust with sugar. Pour the Marsala and white wine into the dish. Scatter the cinnamon sticks over the pears, then cover the dish loosely with foil.

Bake for about 30 minutes, remove the foil and lower the oven heat to 150°C/300°F Gas 2. Continue to bake for a further 30 minutes until the pears are very tender and slightly shrivelled. Serve warm with their juices and crème fraîche.

Pesche Gratinate con Amaretto
Grilled Peaches with Amaretto

Serves 6

8 ripe peaches

1 vanilla pod

2 tablespoons caster sugar

120 ml (4 fl oz) Amaretto

To serve

crème fraîche

Preheat the oven to 190°C/375°F/Gas 5.

Preheat the char-grill or griddle pan.

Slice the peaches in half and remove the stones, trying to keep the cut as clean as possible. Carefully place the peach halves, cut side down, and grill until each peach half has become slightly charred.

Thinly slice the vanilla pod lengthways and put into a mortar with the sugar. Pound with the pestle until broken up and combined.

Place the peach halves face up in a shallow ovenproof baking dish.

Scatter the vanilla sugar over the peaches and pour in some of the Amaretto. Place in the preheated oven and bake for 10 minutes or until the peaches are soft. Pour over the remaining Amaretto and serve hot or cold with crème fraîche.

Torta di Pere e Mandorle
Pear and Almond Tart

Serves 10-12

350 g (12 oz) plain flour

a pinch of salt

175 g (8 oz) unsalted cold butter, cut into cubes

100 g (4 oz) icing sugar

3 egg yolks

For the filling

350 g (12 oz) unsalted butter, softened

350 g (12 oz) caster sugar

350 g (12 oz) blanched whole almonds

3 eggs

6 ripe Comice pears, peeled and halved

For the sweet pastry, pulse the flour, salt and butter in a food processor until the mixture resembles coarse breadcrumbs. Add the sugar then the egg yolks and pulse. The mixture will immediately combine and leave the sides of the bowl. Remove, wrap in cling film and chill for at least an hour. Preheat the oven to 180°C/350°F/Gas 4.

Coarsely grate the pastry into a 30 cm (12 in) loose-bottomed fluted flan tin, then press it evenly on to the sides and base. Bake blind for 20 minutes until very light brown. Cool, and place in the pears, face down. Reduce the oven temperature to 150°C/300°F/Gas 3.

For the filling, cream the butter and sugar until the mixture is pale and light. Put the almonds in a food processor and chop until fine. Add the butter and sugar and blend, then beat in the eggs one by one. Pour over the pears and bake for for 40 minutes.

Torta di Cioccolato e Mandorle
Bitter Chocolate Almond Torte

This cake comes from Capri. It is important that the chocolate be 70 per cent cocoa butter.

Serves 8-10

225 g (8 oz) blanched whole almonds

225 g (8 oz) bitter chocolate, broken into pieces

225 g (8 oz) unsalted butter, softened

225 g (8 oz) granulated sugar

6 medium (or 4 large) eggs, separated

Preheat the oven to 150°C/300°F/Gas 2.

Butter a 20 cm (8 in) deep round spring-release cake tin, and line the bottom with greaseproof paper.

Coarsely grind the almonds in a food processor, and then the chocolate.

Cream the butter and sugar together in an electric mixer, until pale and light. Add the egg yolks one by one, then the ground nuts and chocolate.

Beat the egg whites separately until they form soft peaks. Fold about a quarter into the stiff chocolate mixture to loosen it a little, then fold this mixture into the remaining egg whites.

Put into the prepared tin and bake in the preheated oven for 45 minutes until set. Test by inserting a skewer; if the torte is cooked it will come out clean.

Torta di Castagne e Cioccolato
Chestnut and Chocolate Torte

Serves 8-10

500 g (18 oz) vacuum-packed chestnuts

300 ml (10 fl oz) milk

120 g (4.1/2 oz) whole blanched almonds

150 g (5 oz) best-quality bitter chocolate

120 g (4.1/2 oz) unsalted butter

250 g (9 oz) caster sugar

5 eggs, separated

zest of 1 lemon

For the topping

150 g (5 oz) best-quality bitter-sweet chocolate, melted

with 1 tablespoon unsalted butter

Preheat the oven to 150°C/300°F/Gas 2. Butter a 25 cm (10 in) round spring-release cake tin and line the bottom with greaseproof paper.

Simmer the chestnuts in the milk to soften, about 10 minutes. Drain and discard the milk. Chop the almonds, chocolate and chestnuts together coarsely in a food processor. Cream together the butter and sugar in an electric mixer until pale and light. Add the egg yolks one by one, then the chocolate and nut mixture and the lemon zest.

Beat the egg whites in an electric mixer until they form soft peaks. Fold about a quarter into the stiff chocolate mixture to loosen it a little, then very carefully fold in the remainder. Spoon into the prepared tin and bake in the preheated oven for 45 minutes until the cake has set. When cold, remove from the tin, sit on a rack and cover with the icing.

Crostata di Limone
Lemon Tart

Serves 10-12

1 quantity Sweet Pastry (see page 282)

For the filling

finely grated zest and juice of 7 lemons

350 g (12 oz) caster sugar

6 whole eggs

9 egg yolks

300 g (10 oz) unsalted butter, softened

Preheat the oven to 160°C/325°F/Gas 4.

Press the pastry into the flan tin (see page 282), bake blind, then leave to cool.

Meanwhile, make the filling. Put all the ingredients except the butter in a large saucepan over a very low heat, and whisk until the eggs have broken up and the sugar has dissolved.

Add half the butter and continue to whisk. At this point the eggs will start to cook and the mixture will coat the back of a spoon. Add the remaining butter and continue stirring until the mixture becomes very thick. It is important to continue whisking throughout the cooking process to prevent the mixture from curdling. Remove from the heat, place on a cold surface and continue to whisk until lukewarm.

Raise the oven temperature to 230°C/450°F/Gas 8.

Spoon the lemon filling into the pastry base and bake until the top is brown. This should take about 5-8 minutes.

Torta di Polenta, Mandorle e Limone
Polenta, Almond and Lemon Cake

Serves 10

450 g (1 lb) unsalted butter, softened

450 g (1 lb) caster sugar

450 g (1 lb) ground almonds

2 teaspoons good vanilla essence

6 eggs

zest of 4 lemons

juice of 1 lemon

225 g (8 oz) polenta flour

1.1/2 teaspoons baking powder

1/4 teaspoon salt

Preheat the oven to 160°C/325°F/Gas 3. Butter and flour a 30 cm (12 in) cake tin.

Beat the butter and sugar together until pale and light. Stir in the ground almonds and vanilla. Beat in the eggs, one at a time. Fold in the lemon zest and lemon juice, the polenta, baking powder and salt.

Spoon into the prepared tin and bake in the preheated oven for 45-50 minutes or until set. The cake will be deep brown on top.

Torta di Nocciole e Ricotta
Hazelnut and Ricotta Cake

Serves 10

250 g (9 oz) shelled hazelnuts

250 g (9 oz) ricotta cheese

225 g (8 oz) unsalted butter, softened

250 g (9 oz) caster sugar

8 eggs, separated

finely grated zest of 5 lemons

65 g (2.1/4 oz) plain flour

150 g (6 oz) best quality bitter-sweet chocolate, grated

Preheat the oven to 180°C/350°F/Gas 4. Butter a 30 x 5 cm (12 x 2 in) cake tin, and line with greaseproof paper.

Roast the nuts in the oven until their skins are loosened, about 10 minutes. Peel off the skins by rubbing the hot nuts in a tea-towel. Coarsely chop in a food processor. Beat the butter and sugar together in an electric mixer until pale and light. Add the egg yolks one by one. In a separate large bowl beat the ricotta lightly with a fork. Add the lemon zest and chopped nuts. Beat the egg whites until they form soft peaks.

Fold the egg and butter mixture into the ricotta, then sieve in the flour and finally fold in the beaten egg whites. Spoon into the prepared cake tin and bake in the preheated oven for 35 minutes until set.

Remove from the tin, leave for 5 minutes and, whilst still warm, cover with the chocolate, which will immediately melt.

Chocolate Oblivion

This cake has no sugar

Serves 10-12

675 g (1.1/2 lb) best-quality bitter chocolate, broken into pieces

350 g (12 oz) unsalted cold butter, cut into cubes

9 eggs

Preheat the oven to 220°C/425°F/Gas 7. Butter a 30 x 5 cm (12 x 2 in) cake tin, and line it with greaseproof paper.

Melt the chocolate and butter together in a bowl over a pan of hot water until smooth. The bottom of the bowl should not be in contact with the water. Remove the bowl from the pan to cool a little.

Beat the eggs in a bowl over simmering water until they start to thicken. Remove from the heat and continue beating until soft peaks are formed.

Fold half the eggs into the melted chocolate, combine, then fold in the remaining egg mixture.

Pour into the prepared cake tin, cover with buttered foil and place in a bain-marie of very hot water. It is essential, if the cake is to cook evenly, that the water comes up to the rim of the tin. Bake in the oven for 5 minutes, remove the foil and bake for a further 10 minutes until just set.

Allow the cake to cool – it will continue to set as it does so – then turn out on to a plate.

Pressed Chocolate Cake

This is a squashed chocolate soufflé.

Serves 10

400 g (14 oz) best-quality bitter-sweet chocolate, broken into pieces

300 g (10 oz) unsalted butter

10 eggs, separated

225 g (8 oz) caster sugar

4 tablespoons cocoa powder

Preheat the oven to 180°C/350°C/Gas 4. Butter and flour a 30 x 7.5 cm (12 x 3 in) cake tin.

Melt the chocolate with the butter in a bowl over a pan of simmering water – the water should not be allowed to touch the bowl. Remove the bowl from the pan, cool a little, then whisk in the egg yolks. Add the sugar and cocoa powder and mix well.

Beat the egg whites until they form soft peaks. Fold into the chocolate mixture, a third at a time.

Pour the mixture into the prepared cake tin and bake in the oven for approximately 30 minutes or until the cake has risen like a soufflé and is slightly set. Now place on top a plate that fits exactly inside the tin, press down firmly, and weight it. Leave to cool for 30 minutes, then turn out.

Tartufo di Cioccolato
Chocolate Truffle Cake

Serves 10

450 g (1 lb) extra bitter chocolate, broken into pieces

1 litre (1.3/4 pints) double cream, at room temperature

cocoa powder

Line a 25 x 5 cm (10 x 3 in) cake tin with cling film.

Very slowly melt the chocolate in a bowl over a pan of simmering water. It is essential that the water does not touch the bowl and that the chocolate is not stirred. As soon as the chocolate becomes liquid, remove the bowl from the pan. Let the chocolate cool slightly, but do not allow to set.

Whisk the cream in a large bowl until it forms very soft peaks.

Take a large spoonful of the cream and quickly fold it into the chocolate until it is completely combined and there is no white visible, then immediately fold this mixture into the cream, stir to combine and pour into the prepared cake tin. Chill for at least 2 hours before turning out on to a plate. Dust with cocoa powder.

Quince Cheese

quinces

caster sugar

Rub the quinces with a cloth to remove the down. Put them on a baking tray whole (or halved if they are very large). Cover with foil and bake in a low oven, preheated to about 150°C/300°F/Gas 2 for about 1.1/2 hours, although the time will vary according to the size of the quinces. The quinces are cooked when they are soft but the skins remain unbroken.

Remove from the oven, allow to cool until they can be easily handled, cut in half and take out the core and any tough pieces. Push the flesh and skins through a vegetable mill.

Weigh the pulp and put an equal amount of caster sugar into a saucepan. Add the quince pulp and bring to the boil, stirring constantly, until the quince darkens in colour and comes away from the sides of the pan. This could take up to 30 minutes.

When ready, pour out on to a large flat cold plate and leave to set.

Sorbetto d'Arancie Tarocchi
Blood Orange Sorbet

Serves 6

20 blood oranges

caster sugar

2 lemons

Juice all but one of the oranges and measure the volume of liquid. Use half that volume of caster sugar.

Cut the whole lemons and the remaining orange into quarters, removing the pips. Place in a food processor or blender with the sugar and pulse-chop to a liquid. Add the orange juice and pulse once or twice.

Pour into an ice-cream machine and churn until frozen, or freeze in a suitable container.

This should be served on the same day as it is made.

Sorbetto al Limone
Lemon Sorbet

Serves 10

4 whole lemons, quartered

1 kg (2.1/4 lb) caster sugar

5 ripe bananas, peeled

2 litres (3.1/2 pints) fresh lemon juice

Place the lemons, sugar and bananas in a food processor (it is easier to do this in two batches). Pulse until the mixture is coarse with very small bits of lemon peel still visible.

Put this mixture into a large bowl and stir in the lemon juice. Churn in an ice-cream machine until frozen, or freeze in a suitable container.

Sorbetto alla Fragola
Strawberry Sorbet

Serves 8

1.8 kg (4 lb) strawberries, hulled

2 whole lemons, roughly chopped

800-900 g (1.3/4 – 2 lb) caster sugar

juice of 2 lemons

Place the lemon pieces into a food processor or blender with the sugar, and pulse-chop until the lemon and sugar have combined. Pour into a bowl.

Purée the strawberries and add to the lemon. Add about half the lemon juice, taste and add more if necessary – the flavour of the lemon should be intense but not overpower the strawberries.

Pour into an ice-cream machine and churn until frozen, or freeze in a suitable container.

Sorbetto ai Lamponi e
al Vino Rosso
Raspberry and Red
Wine Sorbet

Serves 10

900 g (2 lb) raspberries

250 ml (8 fl oz) Valpolicella

2 tablespoons lemon juice

100 g (4 oz) caster sugar

50 ml (2 fl oz) double cream

Place all the ingredients in a food processor or blender, and pulse-chop to a liquid.

Pour into an ice-cream machine and churn until frozen, or freeze in a suitable container.

Sorbetto alla Pera e Grappa
Pear and Grappa Sorbet

Serves 10

  1.8 kg (4 lb) very ripe Comice or
    William pears, peeled and cored

  2 tablespoons caster sugar

  2 vanilla pods, split lengthways

  150 ml (5 fl oz) grappa

  juice of 2 lemons

Cook the pears in a pan with the sugar, vanilla pod and 250 ml (8 fl oz) water until soft. Drain. Add the grappa and lemon juice. Push through a very fine sieve, then let cool.

Put into an ice-cream machine and churn until frozen, or freeze in a suitable container.

Sorbetto al Campari
Campari Sorbet

Serves 10

  1 litre (1.3/4 pints) grapefruit juice

  400 g (14 oz) caster sugar

  200 ml (7 fl oz) Campari

  juice of 2 lemons

  juice of 2 oranges

Whisk together the grapefruit juice and the sugar. Add the Campari, lemon and orange juices.

Churn in an ice-cream machine until frozen, or freeze in a suitable container.

Gelato alla Vaniglia
Vanilla Ice Cream

Serves 10

1.75 litres (3 pints) double cream

450 ml (15 fl oz) milk

4 fresh vanilla pods, split lengthways

15 egg yolks

350 g (12 oz) caster sugar

In a large heavy saucepan combine the cream and milk. Scrape the vanilla seeds out of the pods into the pan, using a knife, then add the pods. Heat until just below boiling point.

Beat the egg yolks and sugar together slowly for 10 minutes until pale and thick.

Pour a little of the warm cream into the egg yolks and combine. Return to the saucepan and cook gently over low heat, stirring constantly to prevent the mixture curdling. When it has thickened and is almost at boiling point pour into a bowl and cool.

Pour into an ice-cream machine and churn until frozen, or freeze in a suitable container.

Gelato al Caramello
Caramel Ice Cream

Serves 10

1.75 litres (3 pints) double cream

450 ml (15 fl oz) milk

4 fresh vanilla pods, split lengthways

15 egg yolks

350 g (12 oz) caster sugar

For the caramel

275 g (10 oz) caster sugar

120 ml (4 fl oz) water

Follow the instructions for making Vanilla Ice Cream, then strain the custard into a bowl.

To make the caramel, dissolve the sugar in the water in a heavy-bottomed saucepan, then boil until almost black and smoking. Carefully add this to the custard, and stir thoroughly. Leave to cool.

Pour into an ice-cream machine and churn until frozen, or freeze in a suitable container.

Gelato al Cioccolato e Whisky
Chocolate and Whisky Ice Cream

Serves 10

1.75 litres (3 pints) double cream

450 ml (15 fl oz) milk

4 fresh vanilla pods, split lengthways

15 egg yolks

350 g (12 oz) caster sugar

450 g (1 lb) best-quality bitter-sweet
   chocolate, broken into small pieces

200 ml (7 fl oz) whisky

Follow the instructions for making Vanilla Ice Cream opposite until the mixture has thickened. Whilst still warm, add the chocolate and stir until it has melted. Leave to cool, then add the whisky.

Pour into an ice-cream machine and churn until frozen, or freeze in a suitable container.

Gelato al Caffè
Espresso Ice Cream

Serves 10

1.75 litres (3 pints) double cream

450 ml (15 fl oz) milk

4 fresh vanilla pods, split lengthways

15 egg yolks

350 g (12 oz) caster sugar

1 x 225 g (8 oz) jar good quality
   instant coffee

Follow the instructions for making Vanilla Ice Cream opposite until the mixture has thickened. Put the instant coffee into a bowl and add 300 ml (10 fl oz) of the hot custard. Stir until the granules have dissolved. Return this mixture to the saucepan and stir well; it should be a very dark colour. Allow to cool.

Pour into an ice-cream machine and churn until frozen, or freeze in a suitable container.

Gelato allo Zabaione
Zabaglione Ice Cream

Serves 10

10 egg yolks

200 g (10 oz) caster sugar

120 ml (4 fl oz) Bristol Cream sherry

85 ml (3 fl oz) Jamaica rum

450 ml (15 fl oz) double cream

Place the egg yolks and sugar in an electric mixer and beat until light and fluffy, at least 10 minutes. Add half of the sherry and rum, and transfer the mixture to a bowl that will fit over a large saucepan of boiling water. The water should not touch the bowl. Whisk continuously until the mixture comes to the boil – this will take at least 30 minutes.

Stir in the remaining sherry and rum and leave to cool. If you are using an electric ice-cream machine, add the cream and churn. If freezing directly in the freezer, beat the cream to soft peaks, fold into the mixture, then freeze in a suitable container.

Gelato al Limone e Mascarpone
Mascarpone and Lemon Ice Cream

Serves 10

2.25 kg (5 lb) mascarpone cheese

400 g (14 oz) caster sugar

350 ml (12 fl oz) water

6 tablespoons fresh lemon juice

20 large egg yolks

Bring the sugar and water to the boil in a heavy-bottomed saucepan. Add the lemon juice, and stir until a syrup is formed and the sugar has dissolved.

In a bowl beat the egg yolks until pale and light, then add the syrup in a trickle, whisking all the time. Place the bowl over a simmering pan of water – the water must not touch the bowl – and whisk continuously until the mixture is thick and creamy, about 6-8 minutes. Remove from the heat and continue to whisk until cool. Whisk in the mascarpone, and push through a sieve.

Pour into an ice-cream machine and churn until frozen, or freeze in a suitable container.

Chocolate Nemesis

The best chocolate cake ever.

Serves 10-12

675 g (1.1/2 lb) bitter-sweet chocolate, broken into small pieces

10 whole eggs

575 g (1 lb, 5 oz) caster sugar

450 g (1 lb) unsalted butter, softened

Preheat the oven to 160°C/325°F/Gas 3. Line a 20 x 5 cm (12 x 2 in) cake tin with greaseproof paper, then grease and flour it.

Beat the eggs with a third of the sugar until the volume quadruples – this will take at least 10 minutes in an electric mixer.

Heat the remaining sugar in a small pan with 250 ml (8 fl oz) water until the sugar has completely dissolved to a syrup.

Place the chocolate and butter in the hot syrup and stir to combine. Remove from the heat and allow to cool slightly.

Add the warm syrup to the eggs and continue to beat, rather more gently, until completely combined – about 20 seconds, no more. Pour into the cake tin and place in a bain-marie of hot water. It is essential, if the cake is to cook evenly, that the water comes up to the rim of the tin. Bake in the oven for 30 minutes or until set. Test by placing the flat of your hand gently on the surface.

Leave to cool in the tin before turning out

Al dente Literally meaning 'to the tooth', the phrase denotes the proper texture of pasta and risotto rice, soft outside, with a slight resistance to the bite within.

Amaretto This is an apricot kernel liqueur, which came originally from Saronno. We use it in our almond tart recipe, and with grilled peaches.

Anchovies Salted anchovies are one of the principal ingredients at the River Cafe. Pesce Azzurro is the commercial name by which the Italian government groups small fish like anchovies and sardines. Anchovies are graded by size, then salted whole in large barrels or tins of 5-10 kg (11-22 lb) in weight. The best fish are the largest, and they should be red in colour. When a new tin is opened, the salt pack should be dry. The shopkeeper will pick the required amount of anchovies carefully from the tin or barrel with wooden tongs, to prevent moisture spoiling the remainder. They are bought in Italy by the gram.

To prepare salted anchovies, rinse well under cold running water to remove all the salt. Gently remove the spine bones and heads. Pat dry and use immediately or they will turn brown and lose their flavour. If not using straightaway, you should cover them with olive oil.

Tinned anchovies in oil are no substitute.

Arborio, see *Rice*

Artichoke There are a number of varieties of artichoke available, each of which we use in individual recipes.

Violetti have small heads with fierce prickles and pointed buds. They are in season in December and January, and are eaten when young, either raw or braised whole in olive oil and water.

Romani are the large round artichokes most commonly found in Britain. They're good for Carciofi alla Romana (see page 150).

Morellin is another type of artichoke with a small round head, usually sold by the stem with the leaves on. It is delicious raw or sliced for Carciofi Trifolati (see page 148), or blanched whole and used in salads.

Spinosi is an artichoke grown in Sicily and southern Italy, available in November and sometimes earlier. Sold on their stalks, they are good for deep-frying whole as in Carciofi alla Giudea (see page 146).

Mamare are round artichokes, the first to appear on the plant, and always the biggest. They are usually peeled and the hearts sliced and stuffed or fried. In the market in Verona we watched a woman surrounded by huge boxes of these artichokes, peeling them incredibly quickly with three or four deft cuts, and then tossing them into a bowl of lemon juice and water to be sold ready prepared.

Asparagus We use thin asparagus, known in England as sprue. It cooks quickly, and has a wonderful flavour.

Balsamic vinegar, see *Vinegar*

Basil Many varieties of basil are grown, but that which has grown naturally in strong sun will have the best and most intense flavour and perfume. We only use this herb in late spring and summer as greenhouse-grown basil is tougher in texture with a strong aniseed taste. Handle basil carefully: we prefer to tear the leaves.

We seek out suppliers of purple basil: its intense flavour and beautiful colour are wonderful in salads and with grilled vegetables.

Bush basil grows well in southern England: this has leaves more like marjoram which don't need to be chopped, and their flavour is intense. We use them in marinated and grilled pepper dishes.

Bay leaves Loro in Italian, used to season sausages and stock and pork in vinegar.

Beans, see *Borlotti*, *Cannellini* etc.

Borlotti beans A large round bean striped red on pink, hence the name, fagioli scritti (written beans). Now available fresh in the UK in August and September, but usually purchased dried. Borlotti di Lamon are the largest, most superior and most expensive. In shops in Florence and Siena we have seen up to four sizes of borlotti sold in their dried form.

In Piedmont, borlotti beans are cooked overnight in the wood ovens used for pizzas and bread-baking.

Bottarga This is the salted and sun-dried roe of grey mullet and tuna; it can be obtained from Italian speciality shops in the piece or in tins.

(Tuna fish bottarga is less delicate in flavour.) The best bottarga is that which is removed immediately from the fresh fish, membrane intact, then pressed, salted and dried in the sun. The best is found in the market in Caligari, Sardinia – firm and moist, just right to grate.

Spaghetti with mullet bottarga, olive oil and chilli flakes is to be seen on the menu of every restaurant in Sardinia. A salad of finely shaved bottarga with raw fennel, lemon juice and olive oil is a favourite.

Bread At the River Cafe we serve and use pugliese and ciabatta bread. Pugliese is a large round country-style loaf made with sourdough from the previous day's batch. It's often made with a mixture of flours, and has a good texture for bruschetta. Ciabatta, made with olive oil, resembles a slipper in shape. We use it in our bread soups and toasted in slices rubbed with garlic for crostini.

Bruschetta Thickly sliced pugliese or sourdough bread, which is toasted (preferably char-grilled). It is then rubbed lightly with a fresh clove of garlic and doused with a good extra virgin olive oil while still warm. Serve as it is, or with a variety of toppings.

Butter As salt acts as a stabiliser, unsalted butter is more fragile and therefore absorbs more easily the flavours and aromas of other ingredients. We are always looking for the sweet, unsalted, fresh Italian butter which can be difficult to buy in the UK. The French unsalted pure butter from Normandy is similar.

Cannellini beans In July and August, we can buy them fresh in their pods. The bean is slender, long and ivory white. The taste is nutty, the texture creamy, and the beans take up the flavour of strong herbs such as sage and rosemary, garlic and parsley.

When purchasing dried cannellini beans, look carefully at the sell-by date, as old beans have tough skins. They must be soaked for at least 12 hours and cooked gently without any seasonings, with the possible exception of fresh sage, tomato and garlic in the cooking water.

Capers, salted Capers are the flower buds of a shrub native to the Mediterranean. Capers can be eaten raw, the smaller the better, but are usually lightly dried in the sun and then salted. (The seeds are also salted and dried.)

Salted capers from Sicily, particularly those from the island of Pantelleria, are the most delicious as the fresh flavour of these smaller capers seems to be complemented by the salting process rather than drowned by it. We also found excellent salted capers in the market in Caligari, Sardinia, on a recent wine trip.

Capers need to be soaked and rinsed to remove the salt. Place in a sieve, and wash the salt off under a running tap. If not using straightaway, cover with the best wine vinegar you have. The flavour changes, however, when soaked in vinegar.

Carnoroli, see *Rice*

Carpaccio Named after the Venetian painter, carpaccio is very thin slices of raw beef fillet, dressed with lemon juice and extra virgin olive oil.

Cavolo nero A variety of cabbage that grows in Tuscany; we have never seen it in Italy south of Rome. It grows well in England, as we have discovered by giving seeds to one of the organic farmers who grows vegetables for us.

The leaves grow separately up the main stem so can be continuously picked, and will re-grow in the winter and early spring. We have been told that the texture of these big leaves is only perfect after the first frost. They are very dark green in colour, rather than nero, black, and have a strong bitter taste.

Use Savoy cabbage, or another robust green leaf vegetable if cavolo nero is unavailable. Cavolo nero sometimes means red cabbage, but we refer to the dark green variety.

Cheese, see *Dolcelatte*, *Fontina* etc.

Chickpeas Ceci in Italian, chickpeas were brought to Italy from the Middle East. Look for big ones when buying them dry, and check the sell-by date as they become stale. We use them for soups and in some vegetable dishes.

Chillies We use fresh red chillies in many of our recipes, grilling them, and then removing the seeds and skins. We pound them into a paste for Salsa Rossa, or chop them and cover with extra virgin olive oil for Chilli Sauce. Chillies vary in strength – at the beginning of the harvest, they are definitely milder – but if they are not too strong, we add mint or parsley and/or garlic. At the end of the season, when they are very hot, you must remove the inner filament as well as the seeds.

We also use the very small dried chillies

which you can crumble between your fingers. This acts as a seasoning along with salt and pepper.

Chocolate Use bitter, bitter-sweet or extra-bitter chocolate in our recipes; these have the highest percentage of cocoa butter and very little added sugar. Baker's unsweetened (an American type) is the only one with absolutely no sugar added. We use Valrhona chocolate for Nemesis (see page 302).

Cime di rapa A variety of turnip grown in Italy just for its luxuriant growth of green leaves in winter. These have a deliciously bitter taste, and we use them blanched and dressed with olive oil and lemon juice as they do in Rome. Use young turnip tops instead.

Clams Vongole are small clams found on the coast of Italy from Genoa down to Naples. They are oval in shape and very sweet. Spaghetti alle Vongole is found in every restaurant along that coast. In the River Cafe we use small round clams fished off the coasts of Brittany and Ireland which are equally delicious. It is necessary to soak them in changes of water for some time to remove the sand and grit.

Coppa di Parma This is boned shoulder of pork which is rolled and cured with salt, pepper and nutmeg, then aged for about three months. The perfect coppa from Parma has the same sweet taste as the prosciutto, but consists of equal fat and lean. We use it to wrap beef fillets for Manzo in Tegame (see page 226) and to lard the breasts of game birds. It's also excellent sliced thinly over a rocket salad.

Cotechino This is a spiced pork sausage, a speciality of Emilia-Romagna and Modena. It is made like salami, with both fat and lean pork, cloves, cinnamon and pepper; this mixture is pushed into large skins and cured for a few weeks rather than months. It is available fresh in Italy, but we buy them ready cooked. We serve them hot, particularly in Bollito Misto.

Créme fraîche A thick cream which is partially soured. We like to use it as it is less rich than double cream and does not separate in cooking. You can make it by adding 1 tablespoon soured cream or buttermilk to 300 ml (10 fl oz) double cream, then heating to 30°C (85°F) and leaving it to stand in a warm place for 6-8 hours.

Crostini A toasted slice of ciabatta bread, with a variety of toppings. We put crostini in many of our soups.

Dolcelatte A soft creamy cheese made from cows' milk, with blue-green veins like Gorgonzola, and aged for two months only. It is milder than Gorgonzola.

Fava (broad) beans In parts of Italy, small, young broad beans are eaten raw in their pods with Pecorino cheese.

We use them fresh, out of their pods, cooked with mint and mashed with olive oil, and in Vignole. Dried fava beans are good in soup. Soak as for borlotti beans.

Fennel A very Italian vegetable as it was developed in Italy around the seventeenth century, thus the name Florence fennel. Buy plump, white bulbs, and use the fronds of herb at the top in Salsa Verde.

Fennel herb is a wild plant, which grows all over Italy. It is known as the fish herb and has a much more pronounced aniseed flavour. The leaves and the seeds are both used. Dried fennel herb stalks can be placed under the fish to be baked in the oven.

Flour We use the Italian wheat flour, Tipo 'oo', a white flour which we buy from a miller in Piedmont who still grinds his grain with stone wheels. We use it for making pasta and pizza dough.

Fontina A semi-soft cows' milk cheese from Valle d'Aosta, which is made in large round shapes, and aged for up to five months. It melts easily and has a creamy nutty taste. We use it in a soup of the region along with cabbage and anchovies.

Garlic One of the most essential ingredients in Italian cooking. It is important to choose the heads carefully.

Grappa An Italian eau de vie made from the lees of wine grapes after pressing. It is distilled throughout the hills and mountains of northern Italy and Tuscany, and home-made grappa is on offer in many restaurants in the Alps and Dolomites. It is now also available from the great wine-makers in all regions of Italy.

Grappa Giovane is a young grappa kept in stainless steel after distillation. It is clear in colour and concentrated in taste, retaining the grape characteristics.

Grappa Invecchiata is an aged grappa. Keeping it for years in wooden casks gives it an amber colour and makes it softer and smoother.

Grappa di Mono Vitigno is made from a single grape variety, usually a strongly perfumed grape such as Moscato (Muscat). This grappa is a favourite at the River Cafe: poured over ice cream or into an espresso coffee, it makes a perfect ending to an Italian meal.

Gorgonzola A cows' milk cheese with blue mould streaks. These are made by pricking the forming cheese with copper wires to expose the interior to air and natural moulds. The more holes made, the more pungent the cheese will be. Many are still farm-made and aged in caves in Alpine valleys, in Lombardy, for about two months. Gorgonzola is used, like Dolcelatte, with polenta and pasta. It has a stronger flavour than Dolcelatte.

Herbs, see *Basil, Marjoram, Mint* etc.

Josephine Dore A light unfortified wine from Marsala (Sicily), but it is not a Marsala. Its characteristics are high alcohol, a rich full flavour and dryness. It is very similar to a dry white port.

Lentilles du Puy The best lentils – sold as

lentilles du Puy – are small and coloured from green-brown to blue. They are now grown in Italy as well as in France, where they are known as Castelluccio lentils. They should be available in health-food shops, delicatessens and some good supermarkets. We use them simply dressed with olive oil as an accompaniment to grilled sea bass or mullet: occasionally we add chopped fresh herbs. Boiled lentils form part of the famous Bollito Misto served at New Year, and each part of the dish has a symbolic reference to the year to come: the lentils bring wealth, the meats good health, and the mostarda di Cremona lively spirits.

Luganega sausage The famous Italian sausage, made with coarsely ground pork, is lightly spiced and sometimes has Parmesan in it. The best come from Lombardy. We use them out of their skins in pasta sauces. They are delicious grilled whole and served with tomato sauce and wet polenta

Marjoram Marjoram has a sweeter scent than its wild relation, oregano. We pound the leaves with sea salt to make a salmoriglio sauce for fish. A Sicilian version of the sauce pounds dried and fresh marjoram with olive oil and salt.

Marsala A fortified wine from Sicily, mostly used in the making of zabaglione. It can be sweet or dry.

Mascarpone A fresh, thick cream cheese, originally from Lombardy and Piedmont, made with cows' milk. In Britain it is only available pasteurised, but in Italy you can buy it farm-produced. Serve it as a pudding mixed with double cream, egg whites and sugar.

We use it in sauces, and stuff a mixture of mascarpone and rosemary under the skin of chickens before pan-roasting them.

Mint Mint is known as the herb of Rome, and is traditionally part of the stuffing for artichokes in Carciofi alla Romana. True wild mint – nepitella or mentuccia – is difficult to find in Britain, but it grows everywhere in Italy. We use young tender mint leaves in dishes of fresh and wild mushrooms, in salads, and scattered over deep-fried zucchini. Mint is an essential ingredient of Salsa Verde.

Mostarda di Cremona Also called mostarda di frutta, this is a piquant preserve which is traditionally served with the boiled meats of Bollito Misto. It is made of candied fruits such as peaches, apricots, pears, figs and cherries, which are preserved in a honey, white wine and mustard syrup.

When the late Elizabeth David came to the River Cafe, she told us of a stall in the Venice market where you could buy home-made mostarda. We have yet to track it down.

Mozzarella di bufala Between Rome and Naples, along the Latium coast, water buffalo still graze in the fields, and farm shops will sell you true buffalo milk mozzarella. These are rather larger than the ones you can normally buy, and they are fairly rare. We are very lucky to have a supplier who flies buffalo mozzarella into London from Naples twice a week, as the cheeses must be eaten very fresh, no more than three days old. We serve the cheese whole; this gives you the pleasure of cutting into it, still dripping with its own buttermilk

Many mozzarellas are made with cows' milk so check the wrapping paper.

Olives In Italy everybody has their own olives preserved in brine. In Tuscany the olives are usually quite small and coloured purple and green; the brine is often flavoured with wild fennel stalks and seeds. We wash off the brine and marinate the olives in olive oil with tiny dried chillies, dried oregano and pieces of garlic.

The large green, purple, yellow and brown olive from Sicily, the Nocellano de Belice, is a new and delicious addition to our range of tastes. The sleek, pointed, purple-black Calamata olive from Greece is a favourite for use in olive sauces, as its flavour is so strong, salty and distinctive.

Olive oil In every part of Italy olive oil is the basis of cooking. We have at least three varieties on the go at any one time in the River Cafe. We use a lighter oil for frying, such as the Ligurian oil; this is pressed from olives that have ripened on the trees, so the oil is gentler in flavour and paler in colour, ideal for Fritto Misto and deep-fried zucchini flowers. Thick green fruity oils from Tuscany are wonderful added to bread soups. And the dense and fruity olive oil from Ornellaia is marvellous for salad as its quality seems to be constant throughout the year. The only blended extra virgin olive oil we use is in the initial preparation of soups and vegetables.

Olive oil is a seasonal product, and when first harvested in November has a completely different taste and colour. Sometimes a new oil is so peppery and hot that it can burn your tongue and palate like a chilli. New oil poured over hot bruschetta is a gastronomic experience we look forward to every year, for now that our reputation has spread, we are invited to Italy to taste the new oils. We have tried oils pressed in the newest, most mechanised presses, and those pressed in traditional water-run stone-ground mills.

Onions, Red We use red onions, as we prefer their sweet, more delicate flavour. The original Panzanella, a peasant dish, was made of onions, bread and olive oil.

Oregano Oregano is a wild version of marjoram, and is the only herb that is used dry more frequently than it is fresh. It is used dried in pizzas and tomato sauces. Fresh oregano has a strong peppery edge to its flavour.

Pancetta Pancetta is basically a streaky bacon, coming from the belly of pork. Pancetta stesa is cured for about three weeks and then is hung to air-dry for up to four months. Pancetta stesa is widely used in the Italian kitchen, and it has a depth of flavour that cannot be equalled by any streaky bacon. A leaner pancetta is rolled and tied – arrotolata – and flavoured with herbs, cloves, nutmeg, salt, pepper, garlic and sometimes fennel seeds, and then air-dried as well. A smoked pancetta, affumicata, comes from the Alto Adige, Valle d'Aosta and Friuli regions; it is usually fattier.

Panettone A northern Italian, dome-shaped cake made with yeast and dried and candied fruit. It was traditionally given as a gift at Christmas, and eaten as a Christmas cake, but it is now enjoyed up to Easter. It can be bought in different sizes at Italian delicatessens, or you can make it yourself from a good recipe.

Parmesan Known as Parmigiano in Italy, the cheese is actually a grana, a hard and grainy, pressed cheese made from partially skimmed cows' milk. Parmigiano Reggiano from Emilia is regarded as the best. The cheeses are shaped like huge wheels, and can be aged for over two years. A younger Parmesan – a nuovo – is good as a dessert cheese with fruit, or flaked or slivered on top of salads; an older Parmesan, which is harder – a vecchio or a stravecchio – is grated on to soups, pasta etc.

Parsley We use only flat-leaf parsley as it has a more definite taste and texture than the curly. We use heaps of it every day in the restaurant, in soups, sauces and vegetable dishes. Chopped with onion, celery and carrots, it forms soffritto, the base of Ribollita and Minestrone.

Pasta, see page 59

Pecorino This ewes' milk cheese is made all over Italy, and can be soft when young, hard when pressed and matured. Pecorino toscano, although not well known, is an essential ingredient in Tuscan cooking; there the cheeses are small and round, made with differing flavoured milk, depending on where the sheep have been grazing – mountain, hill or seaside –

and the varying herbs they have ingested. Some of these local Pecorinos are eaten fresh, some are kept for about six months. We use these latter cheeses for grating over pasta and adding to pesto.

Pecorino from Piedmont is nearly always very fresh and delicate, with a light taste, and is eaten on its own. Pecorino romano is the best known, larger, stronger and more mature than its Sardinian cousin Pecorino sardo. Both have very strong distinctive tastes.

Pecorino siciliano sometimes has peppercorns added to it, and it is delicious eaten fresh. The aged hard version is also delicious with olives and olive oil from the same region.

When broad beans are fresh and young, it is traditional in Tuscany to eat them whole in their pods with Pecorino and the local olive oil.

Peppercorns, black As we like our black pepper very coarse, we pound the peppercorns in a pestle and mortar. Pepper loses its flavour very quickly once it is crushed, so we do just enough for service each day.

Polenta, see page 119

Porcini Porcini – 'little pigs' in Italian – are ceps, or *Boletus edulis*. The season for fresh mushrooms is very short – September and October – but many are dried, which concentrates the flavour so much that porcini are used almost like a seasoning. When buying dried porcini, look for large and meaty, creamy brown sections; avoid dark brown crumbly pieces. Store them in an airtight container, and never replace them with fresh mushrooms in a recipe.

Dried porcini must be reconstituted before use. Soak them in warm to hot water for 15-20 minutes. Keep the soaking water which will be dark brown and intensely flavoured; pass this through a fine muslin or a filter to get rid of any grit, and add the liquid to the porcini as they cook (depending on the recipe). Rinse the porcini themselves after soaking to get rid of any remaining grit, then pat dry and use as directed in the recipes.

Potatoes We have spent a lot of time trying to find the equivalent of the delicious Italian yellow waxy potato that is sold in every greengrocer in Tuscany. A few varieties come close, and they are available in shops and supermarkets.

Linska is grown for us by one of our suppliers, and is a large yellow, oval-shaped potato that we use in late summer for slicing and baking with sage or pancetta, or balsamic vinegar and red onions.

Roseval is a French potato with a red skin and yellow waxy flesh streaked with pink. It too is good for slicing and baking. Often kidney-shaped, the larger the potato the better the flavour.

Charlotte is very similar to Linska. These are oval and are perfect for deep-frying.

We also occasionally use *Ratte* potatoes, another French variety with a delicious taste and waxy texture.

Prosciutto Prosciutto is the Italian word for ham. There are several types, but two are particularly important, our own first choice being San Daniele.

Prosciutto di San Daniele is salted and air-dried for about twelve months, always with the trotter attached. It is made in the Friuli region, where the pigs feed in the fields and oak woods. The meat is very lean, and the flavour pronounced.

Prosciutto di Parma – also known as prosciutto crudo, raw ham, or, in Britain, Parma ham – is salted and air-dried as well. The pigs are kept in huts, and fed on the whey left over from the making of the local Parma cheese, Parmesan, as well as on local grain. The meat is sweeter and more fatty than San Daniele.

If you buy prosciutto in the piece, you are sometimes left with the hock or the end pieces which are difficult to slice. We use them in soups and stocks, and for sausages.

Rice Three risotto rices grown in the Po Valley in the north of Italy are commonly available in Britain, arborio, vialone and carnoroli, the latter being our own first choice. These types of rice have plump long grains, and more starch than other rice types, and they will therefore withstand the longer slower cooking necessary to properly infuse risotto with the particular flavour you are after. As the rice cooks, starch is released which gives the risotto its creamy texture; the centre of the rice grain remains slightly firm to the teeth – al dente – which is what give risotto its unique texture.

Ricotta Ricotta is a fresh 'cheese' made from the re-cooked whey of milk separated for cheese-making (usually Pecorino or mozzarella).

It is actually a *by-product* of cheese, not really a cheese in itself. It can be made from buffalos', cows' or sheeps' milk; a goats' milk ricotta is made at Parma. The curds are shaped in traditional baskets. All varieties only last for two to four days.

Piedmontese ricotta is made from cows' milk, and is very creamy. It is usually eaten with sugar. Ricotta Romana is made with sheeps' milk. Ricotta salata is Sicilian, salted and dried in the sun. Ricotta di bufala, the most rare and delicate of all, comes from Naples, and we have it flown in especially. We serve it with honey. It is equally good with extra virgin olive oil and a rocket salad.

Cows' milk ricotta made in England is widely available.

Rocket Rocket is a peppery salad leaf plant known also as rucola, rughetta, arugula and roquette. The size of the leaf varies, but the more mature and the bigger the leaves are, the better and stronger the taste. Rucola di Capri is a wild rocket with very small leaves, more like a herb than a salad plant.

Use as soon as possible, washing it well and discarding yellowed leaves and tough stems.

Rosemary Rosemary grows all around the Mediterranean, in hedges and wind-breaks, and in the wild. It has an intense aromatic flavour and perfume. We use it mostly with meat.

Sage Sage is a pungent herb often cooked with calves' liver. We always put sage leaves into the cooking water of borlotti or cannellini beans. Fresh sage leaf 'sandwiches', with a salted

anchovy in the middle, deep-fried, make a brilliant addition to Fritto Misto. Sage also flavours a butter for ravioli.

Salt, Sea We use two kinds of salt in the restaurant. Maldon sea salt, which has large brittle crystals, for seasoning. It has no additives, and is concentrated in its natural form. Coarse sea salt has very large grains, and we use this in the cooking water of pasta and vegetables. We also pack this around whole salmon or sea bass when baking them in the oven; the large grains do not dissolve as the fish cooks and seal in the juices.

Sausages, see *Cotechino*, *Luganega*, *Zampone* etc.

Squid or cuttlefish ink If you clean the fish yourself, be careful to preserve the ink sacs to use in recipes. A good fishmonger should be able to sell you small sachets of ink to be used in fish sauces or in a 'black' risotto (see page 114).

Tarragon This distinctive herb is difficult to find in Italy, only seeming to appear in Florence and Siena. We like to use it in a sauce with boiled meats.

Tomatoes, fresh There is a huge variety of tomatoes available in Italy.

Plum tomatoes – San Pier Cuore di Bue – are ripened on the vine. They are very juicy and deep red in colour, so are ideal for cooking. They are only available from July until October.

Costuluto Fiorentina is a large salad tomato,

and ripens to a reddish green colour. Beef tomatoes are a poor substitute.

Tiny Tuscan vine tomatoes – Agrapolo Bombolino – hang in tresses like grapes. Burst them on to a piece of bruschetta that has been rubbed with garlic, sprinkle with sea salt and douse with olive oil.

Small cherry tomatoes are good for raw tomato sauce as their flavour is sweeter and stronger than the plum.

If you cannot get hold of a good tomato, use tinned plum tomatoes, which are much better than inferior fresh ones. We use tinned tomatoes all year round.

Tomatoes, sun-dried Buy dried tomatoes – pomodori secchi – dry, and not in olive oil or any other liquid. Soak them in water for at least 2-3 hours to rehydrate them, then drain. Use in recipes or pat dry and marinate in extra virgin olive oil with dried oregano, pepper and salt.

Trevise The proper name for this winter vegetable is radicchio rosso di Treviso. It comes from an area in the north, around Venice and Treviso, and when cooked is not as bitter as its round relative, the more familiar red radicchio di Chioggia. The leaves are long and pointed and they grow in bunches.

Vinegar Aceto balsamico, or balsamic vinegar, has been made in Modena for many centuries, during which time the production method has hardly changed. Fresh grape juice is boiled in an open pot over fire for at least a day, after which the liquid is transferred to wooden vats for ageing. This ageing varies from a couple of

years for the cheapest commercial products, through to twelve and fifteen years for the middle price range, and up to fifty years for the outrageously expensive. The older the vinegar, the darker in colour it is, and the more intensely sweet. Most *balsamici* are blends of young vinegars with a small amount of the very old concentrated one.

We choose a red wine vinegar made by the wine producer Allegrini whose wines we know and sell. Aceto Cortegiara is a smooth red vinegar traditionally made from Veronese wines, and aged for three years in small oak casks that previously held brandy.

Vongole, see Clams

Vermouth A flavoured white wine made on both sides of the Alps in France and Italy. Alpine herbs and various other bitter flavourings are macerated or cooked in the wine. Choose the driest you can find for adding to risottos.

Zampone A speciality of Modena, spiced pure pork is stuffed into a boned pig's trotter. It is sold fresh in Italy, but part-cured for export. It is traditionally served with dried beans or lentils or part of the great Bollito Misto.

Zucchini Italian and American word for courgette.

Suppliers of Italian Foods

London area

R. Allens & Co. Butchers
117 Mount Street
London W1Y 6HX
tel: 0171 499 5831

Carluccio's
28a Neal Street
London WC2H 9PS
tel: 0171-240 1487
(0171-240 5710 for local stockists)

Camisa & Son
61 Old Compton Street
London W1 5BN
tel: 0171-437 7610

Clarke's
124 Kensington Church Street
London W8
tel: 0171 221 9225

Gastronomia Italia
8 Upper Tachbrook Street
London SW1V 1SH
tel: 0171-834 2767

Giacobazzi's
150 Fleet Road
London NW3 2QX
tel: 0171-267 7222

Harvey Nichols
Knightsbridge
London SW1X 7RJ
tel: 0171 235 5000

Italy Si (mail order)
Unit 3, 199 Eade Road
London N4 1DN
tel: 0181-442 8218

L Terroni & Sons
St Peter's House
138/140 Clerkenwell Road
London EC1R SDL
tel: 0171-837 1712

La Fromagerie
30 Highbury Park
London N5 2AA
tel: 0171 359 7440

Lidgates Butchers
110 Holland Park
London W11 4UA
tel: 0171 727 8243

Lina Stores
18 Brewer Street
London W1R 3FS
tel: 0171-437 6482

Luigi's
349 Fulham Road
London SW10 9TW
tel: 0171-352 7739

Panzer
13–19 Circus Road
London NW8 6PB
tel: 0171 722 8596

Tom's
226 Westbourne Grove
London W11 2RH
tel: 0171 221 8818

Winecellars
153/155 Wandsworth High Street
London SW18 4JB
tel: 0181 871 3979

Outside London

A. Di Maria & Son
588 Foleshill Road
Coventry CV6 5HP
tel: 01203-687968

Cibo Continental Ltd
289 Gloucester Road
Horfield, Bristol BS7 8NY
tel: 01179 429475

Europa Food Store
78 Hampthill Road
Bedford MK42 9HP
tel: 01234 352626

Fratelli Sarti
133 Wellington Street
Glasgow G2 2XD
tel: 0141 2487794

Gastromania
1 Brewery Court
Cirencester
Glos GL7 1JH
tel: 01285-644611

Italian Continental Stores
Vicarage Road
Maidenhead
Berks SL6 78L
tel: 01628-77040

The Italian Shop
51 Cathays Terrace
Cardiff
tel: 01222-232677

The Little Vine Yard
113A Unthank Road
Norwich NR2 2PE
tel: 01603-621704

Pasquale Vincenzo
115 Derby Road
Loughborough LE11 OAE
tel: 01509-212786

Paul Ceci Delicatessen
59 Wylds Lane
Worcester WR5 1DA
tel: 01905-353602

Ramsbottom Victuallers Co Ltd
16-18 Market Place
Ramsbottom
Lancs BLO 9HT
tel: 01706-825070

Roma Delicatessen
268 Bury Old Road
Whitefield
Manchester M25 6oS
tel: 0161 766 2941

Silver Palate
3 Vaughan Road
Harpenden
Herts ALS 4HU
tel: 01582-713722

Valvona & Crolla Ltd
19 Elm Row
Edinburgh EH7 4AA
tel: 0131-556 6066

What's for Dinner? Ltd
23 Market Place
Henley-on-Thames
Oxon RG9 2AA
tel: 01491-412128

Most of the larger supermarkets
stock a good range of Italian foods.

Index

The authors would like to thank: Lucy Boyd, Sam Clark, Theo Randall, Lucia Bartolini, Dada Rogers, Michael Elias, Jan Hall, Hester Gray, Francesca Melman, Fiorenza Bartolini, Eamon O'Mahony, Ossian Gray, Sylvia Elias, Steven Evennett-Watts, Johnathon Burnham, Richard Rogers, David MacIlwaine, Susan Fleming, Susan Elias, Jake Hodges, David Gleave, Chloe Peploe, Judith Hannan, David Eldridge, James Merrell, Sheila Hale, Adam Alavarez, Kathy Botts, Ed Victor, Jason Creagh, Fiona MacIntyre, John Brown, Ricky Burdett, Renzo Bentsik, Jane Baxter, Bo Rogers, Roo Rogers, Dante MacIlwaine Gray, All Staff past and present at the River Cafe.